On Following Jesus

Books Published

Biblical Hermeneutics: An Introduction

Called to Teach: The Vocation of the Presbyterian Educator, editor with William J. Weston

Exploring the Spirituality of the World Religions: The Quest for Personal, Spiritual, and Social Transformation

Living Wisely and Well in the Evening of Life: Foundations for Flourishing; A Spiritual Perspective

Lovescapes: Mapping the Geography of Love; An Invitation to the Love-Centered Life

Making the Bible Your Book: Content and Interpretation

Mindful Spirituality: The Intentional Cultivation of the Spiritual Life; A Book of Readings

New Age Spirituality: An Assessment, editor

The Radical Invitation of Jesus: How Accepting the Invitation of Jesus Can Lead to Living Faith and Fulfilling Life for Today

The Radical Teaching of Jesus: A Teacher Full of Grace and Truth; An Inquiry for Thoughtful Seekers

The Teachers of Spiritual Wisdom: Gaining Perspective on Life's Perplexing Questions, with Jamal Rahman and Mary Petrina Boyd

The Human Odyssey: The Journey of the Soul in Perilous Times

Traces of Transcendence: The Heart of the Spiritual Quest

Elias Chacour, *The Sermon on the Mount: An Invitation to Receive and Advance the Reign of God*, editor

"*On Following Jesus* drives the reader to ponder a salient question: what could it mean to have God at the center of one's attention as one engages a troubled and unnerving world? Duncan Ferguson makes an appeal for readers to consider the way of Jesus as offering a fulfilling, humane, and loving answer. This is a psychologically astute, biblically focused, and theologically learned book, a compelling account by a respected and wise author."

—Mark Valeri, The Reverend Priscilla Wood Neaves Distinguished Professor of Religion and Politics in the John C. Danforth Center for Religion and Politics, Washington University in St. Louis

"*On Following Jesus* offers a culmination of the author's faith journey, academic posts, and previous books. This well-researched book glimpses Jesus as healer, teacher, and prophet. Dr. Ferguson embodies the mind of Jesus in his own life of commitment, openness, attentiveness to the world as it is at present, and hope based on the values of Jesus: truth, love, justice, and peace. Dr. Ferguson is vulnerable as he deals with the challenges of ministry where love in action is needed. Several sections cover practical aspects of following Jesus: faith development, compassionate communication at the end of life, and key scriptural passages explained clearly. This book is an essential resource in troubled times giving readers a framework for spirituality and service reflecting the heart and mind of Jesus."

—Lorraine Stuart, Spiritual Director, Honorably Retired, Cascades Presbytery

"An effective treatment plan for the spiritual ills of the contemporary situation! Ferguson invites us to look to the historical Jesus for the mindset and skills we need to navigate the perilous present. If you need a healing balm that is simultaneously a set of marching orders, look no further."

—Gordon S. Mikoski, Associate Professor of Christian Education, Princeton Theological Seminary

"This exceptional book is truly precious and inspiring. It combines rigorous scholarship with deep spiritual wisdom. The author's exploration of the life and ministry of Jesus is both compelling and transformative. Accessible to readers of all faiths, it encourages a God-centered life grounded in truth, love, justice, and peace."

—Jamal Rahman, author of *Spiritual Gems of Islam*

On Following Jesus

Let This Heart and Mind Be in You

DUNCAN S. FERGUSON

WIPF & STOCK · Eugene, Oregon

ON FOLLOWING JESUS
Let This Heart and Mind Be in You

Wipf & Stock
An Imprint of Wipf and Stock Publishers
199 W. 8th Ave., Suite 3
Eugene, OR 97401

www.wipfandstock.com

PAPERBACK ISBN: 979-8-3852-6512-1
HARDCOVER ISBN: 979-8-3852-6513-8
EBOOK ISBN: 979-8-3852-6514-5

Dedicated to those who diligently follow the way of Jesus in an informed, engaged, and faithful way.

Contents

Introduction

Let This Same Heart and Mind Be in You That Was in Christ Jesus

Again, Jesus spoke to them, saying, "I am the light of the world. Whoever follows me will never walk in darkness, but will have the light of the world."

—John 8:12

Jesus said to him, "I am the way, and the truth, and the life."

—John 14:6

I AM WRITING IN the time of Donald Trump's second term as president of the United States. It is a profoundly confusing and difficult time for me and many of the citizens of the United States.[1] It is also a somewhat confusing time for the leaders and citizens of many other countries, in part because one of the best ways of addressing their country's needs has been to take advantage of the resources of the United States and to cultivate a collaborative and trustworthy partnership. These linkages are currently being reviewed and questioned.[2]

1. There have been major demonstrations in every state of the union about the direction of our federal government.

2. President Zelenskyy of Ukraine has had a difficult relationship with President Trump, and Russia continues its attack on Ukraine. I wouldn't be surprised if many countries are feeling betrayed by the financial policies set in place by Donald Trump.

It is a connection that is often financial in character, although deep down it is more than just financial. It is also about how to secure a safe, good, and peaceful life for their citizens by collaborating with the United States in the quest to be safe from external threats and to increase financial stability for the benefit of their citizens. In many cases, the connection with the United States has ensured a more just society and enabled these countries to help create a humane and compassionate context in which to live, yet this positive assumption about the relationship may now not be altogether accurate.[3]

Many of the early initiatives, decisions, and actions of Donald Trump and his array of insiders have made many people, both in the United States and in many countries of the world, wonder whether this presidential team can guide and empower the United States and its partners to move toward a safe and secure future. The quite dramatic decisions being made continue to cause threatening shifts to the way of life that is valued in the United States by many political leaders and a large percentage of its citizens. Most of these leaders use the language of the loss of democracy and the rise of autocracy. They oppose having a king! Many of the appointments President Trump has made to serve by his side in his cabinet and in the several phases of national life are seen as lacking adequate experience to manage their area of responsibility. The decisions and changes he has made, partially influenced by those who were close to him, have raised alarming questions about our future.[4]

From the beginning of the second term of the Trump presidency, thoughtful and experienced people in our government have been concerned about inadequate leadership for the basic running of the federal government and its many areas of responsibility. They have also worried that many of these areas of government responsibility may be reduced or eliminated, causing extensive job losses and the elimination of a component of the government that does vital work for our nation, especially in serving the poor and the sick. In addition, many areas and organizations that serve the foundational needs of the country, such as universities and health care organizations, are being threatened.

3. Canada is deeply offended by Donald Trump's suggestion that Canada become the fifty-first state of the United States.

4. See the article by Yale historian Timothy Snyder entitled "The Logic of Destruction," which describes the current federal administration under Donald Trump as inherently serf-serving and dangerous. There is extensive research being done and the publications on the subject are numerous.

It also appears that the Trump leadership team is paying little attention to the deep threats that already exist.[5] For example, the threat of climate change and its overlap with a deteriorating natural environment is one on everyone's list of threats to a good future. Yet this profound threat may not be getting the attention it needs from the president's leadership team, although it may surface later as the team gains experience. More progressive political leaders who speak about the deep threat to human well-being cannot be discounted by saying that it is just a product of liberals in their "woke" culture. It may be a bit early to predict the future of the United States, influenced as it is by Donald Trump's second term and his team, yet there are certainly enough signals to cause alarm.

The 2024 fire in the Los Angeles area was a signal about threats to the environment, and it suggested that environmental disasters may be just around the corner, not only in California, but also in other parts of the United States and the world. There is also conflict between leaders of regions and the president about the possible entrance of national troops to help address social unrest. The governor of California, while acknowledging the unrest in his state, strongly resisted the entrance of national troops into California, as did the local leadership in Washington, DC.

We ask whether the governments of the world and our government in particular have the capacity to respond adequately to these threats, regardless of whether these threats come in the form of fires, earthquakes, floods, poverty, immigration, hunger, or aggressive self-serving initiatives and violence. These features of the second term of Trump's leadership add intensity to the now common question, "How then shall we live as Americans and, indeed, how should the whole human family live given the range and depth of the problems we face?"

Even those who live day to day in a simple routine of life are being forced to ask the hard questions about their future. It does appear that nearly the whole human family is concerned. All of us are beginning to "catch on" to the threats.[6] I sense in my conversations with thoughtful and informed observers and in watching world news that there is now a global awareness of the threat to the earth's future. For example, there is an existential threat present in the consciousness of those who have walked

5. Almost all of the lists of world problems include poverty, war, and climate change.

6. Research on how the public feels about our current situation reveals a lack of confidence in President Trump and a deep disagreement with the way he is guiding the country. As I write, his approval rating is 36 percent. Maddow, "Anti-Trump Protests."

the trails that lead north from Nicaragua through Mexico and on to the American border, hoping to find a safe life in the United States. Many of these people are being sent back to their country of origin. As they are forced to return, we wonder if their lives would have improved even if they did get into the United States in a legitimate way. There are new entrance requirements in place that make it much more difficult for noncitizens to enter. These new immigrants now see that many of those seekers who have made it in, but who have no formal approval, are being deported. They may also wonder, even if they do gain legitimate status, whether they will be able to find a better a life in United States, especially since there is the presence of all the many problems facing the human family such as the threatening dimensions of climate change. Will making a geographical shift lead to a better life? These travelers may not be aware of the scientific evidence that points to a global crisis such as climate change or ask all the right questions about life in the United States, but they face poverty and have fear about the future in their country of origin and seek a better place to live.

There is also the threat to our finest universities that depend upon government support. In particular, international students who have come to the United States to study may not be able to complete their research and get their degrees if they lose financial aid; it is a current threat. Many of these students are engaged in critical research related to human survival, but have lost their visas and are unable to continue their work.

In addition, medical care in the United States is prohibitively expensive without Medicare or private health insurance, and a severe reduction of these very important programs may have a negative impact on this segment of people in the United States. Further, many in retirement depend on Social Security, another threatened program, which assures those in retirement that they will have adequate income in their retirement years. Both good health and having adequate income are essential for the well-being of the elderly population, a large and increasing segment of the population.

The citizens of the United States are not alone in managing an array of social problems. Fear is global, and informed questions about finding a safe and just social order are being asked with intensity in nearly every corner of the earth. Will India be able to feed its millions of people? What will be Russia's next move or conquest? Will the leaders of North Korea push over the first domino that will take us all down? Will China be willing to work in a cooperative way with other nations of the world? Can Israel be safe from invasion, surrounded as it is by Arab nations? Does it have the right to bomb the people in Gaza? How should the United States be related to current conflict between Israel and Iran? Can the native people of the world continue their traditional way of life? How should we deal with the issues of food distribution around the world and address severe hunger in parts of Africa? Will our children be able to tolerate the poisoned atmosphere as they move into adulthood? Even some of the billionaires from Europe, the Middle East, and the United States are now more fully understanding that their wealth and way of life are threatened by global problems, although President Trump's policies do favor the wealthy.

This relatively new and almost global awareness of dangerous climate change is forcing all of the human family to pause, ponder, and worry. Leaders of governments, presidents of international companies, and those responsible for global farming that feeds the human family are reflecting on the threats to the well-being of the earth. This reflection is not just about how to be more efficient and increase profits; it is also and more importantly about how to take care of the parent of all of us, Mother Earth. The concern is not just about how the government leaders of "first world" countries respond in an informed way to the threat, but it is also about how the whole human family learns how to live in a responsible way, taking into account the range of global threats.

Climate change is not the only threat facing the human family and the well-being of Mother Earth. Just a glance at the list of global problems on Wikipedia is enough to ruin one's sleep. The following concerns are on the recent list[7]:

- Biodiversity loss
- Climate change
- Destructive artificial intelligence
- Nuclear holocaust
- Another pandemic
- Biotechnology risk
- Molecular nanotechnology
- Societal collapse

The United Nations has prepared a comprehensive list of global concerns that include poverty and disease in Africa, the aging of the human

7. Wikipedia, "Global Catastrophic Risk."

family, the use or misuse of atomic energy, difficulty of tracking and supporting sustainable development goals, threats to children worldwide, climate change, decolonization, erosions of democracy, increase of armaments, poverty, shortage of food, gender equality, migration, law and justice, peace and security, terrorism, loss of water, disarmament, and several more.[8] The World Economic Forum lists their "top ten."[9]

So, again, we have our question: how then shall we live? We know that it must be answered with a sense of caring for the earth, living in a responsible way that is fully informed about global threats, and then having the honesty and integrity to care for the welfare of the earth. There is no room for the denial of the severe problems, the challenge of overcoming vested interest, and the costs for taking positive action. This effort must be one that is filled with a commitment to seek justice and a good life for all without the pettiness and prejudices of small minds, the selfish ambition of autocratic leaders, and the vested interests of global companies. There must be compassion for all those who suffer and a united effort of the human family that gives attention to caring for those who are the most threatened. In fact, we all must become those who care about all of life on earth, sensing the interconnection of all that lives, and then find our place in helping to ensure the health of the natural world and a commitment to create a safe and just world. The question for all of us is whether the human family has a frame of reference that enables them to understand the threat and to work with shared values and a realistic outlook. It is both the outlook (frame of reference) and common values that are needed if we are going to be able to manage the earth's future.

Seldom mentioned by those who are resisting change is the word "compassion"; it is not a negative word or a sign of weakness,[10] but one essential key to the human future. It must be a critical component for those who design strategy for the future, yet it is a human quality that is being often ignored and is replaced by the quest for power and financial gain.[11]

8. United Nations, "Global Risk Report." For a discussion of related development goals, see Willige, "Five Years to Go."

9. Hutt, "What Are the 10." On the list are food security, inclusive growth, the future of work/unemployment, climate change, financial crisis (2007–2008), the future of internet, gender equality, global trade, long-term investment strategy, and future health care.

10. It is seen by those with Trump as a weak emotion within those who lack the courage to make difficult changes.

11. Tim Weiner, in his book *The Mission: The CIA in the 21st Century*, makes it very clear that decision-making at the federal level is driven by the uses and abuses of power,

I have neither the knowledge and wisdom nor the authority to speak for the worldwide organizations that are engaged in the work of preserving the health of the earth. I do honor those with a comprehensive perspective and find their descriptions and assessments very informative, although troubling as they identify the problems we face. I am also aware of those countries and global organizations that may have both the knowledge and the power to make change. I support their efforts to find a way into the future that can reduce the range of threats and increase our hope for a safe and secure future. Yet, even with the exception of a few healthy practices in my setting, I am left with only a vague hope that somehow the human family will find a way to create a more just and sustainable future, one that honors the global environment in all of its rich diversity.

What I can and should do, initially, is to look at my own life and begin to understand how I might be a better citizen of my location, the needs of my country, and the threats that exist in nearly all parts of the world. There is an abundance of guidelines available on how to be a responsible citizen of my region, my country, and my world. I do pay attention to these guidelines, a very important first step. Yet I find that I want to do more than just read, be aware, and then be careful about what I buy at the grocery store. But we, the human family, need to go beyond awareness to action. I do hope that I can engage in positive action that will help make the world a bit safer for my grandchildren. There is a need for a well-informed compassion that has an action component. Each of us must find our way to help.

I will try in a way that is natural and possible for me, as we all must do. So, given my history, place in the social context, and my awareness and education, I add to my agenda an exploration of how I might nudge one part of the vast worldwide organization, the ecumenical Christian church, toward continuing to engage in wisely caring for the earth and addressing the many forms of human suffering. I want the worldwide church to go beyond visionary documents, as important as they are, and to use these documents as action plans with clear guidance on how to express compassionate commitment in tangible ways.[12] Perhaps I can make a modest

---

not the ideals of compassion and justice.

12. I will speak of the vast worldwide movement as the church, and then individual expressions of this global movement as part of the mission of a particular church. I will also identify denominations and movements within the church, reference initiatives of denominations, and point to interfaith initiatives and active organizations. An internet search for "Presbyterian views on the climate crisis," for example, illustrates one Christian denomination's theological perspective and pattern of action.

difference in that the church has been my spiritual home for seventy years and I have learned how it functions as a force for compassion, justice, and care for Mother Earth. For the most part, the church is a context in which people are able and willing to learn how to be more responsible and modestly informed about the threats to the environment.

I still have a few connections with its organizations and leaders and believe that I may be heard if I am wise about how I communicate; there is a desire to learn and a sensitive conscience in the church. Yes, there are inconsistencies in this vast worldwide family, some here in the United States that make me cringe, but there are also literally thousands of Christian denominations and organizations and millions of people with resources and a sensitive conscience who care deeply about God's magnificent gift of Mother Earth and the health of all of her children.[13]

As I look around for a place to do my part, I find that I do have friends and acquaintances who have some power and influence in this worldwide organization called the church, which was established to do good in the world. I can start small, share my views, utilize the vast amount of good work that has already been done, and then hope that some other sensitive and spiritual people and organizations might join together in a positive, ecumenical, and inclusive spirit to help create a safe, just, and healthy world. I summarize this need with the title of this book, *On Following Jesus*. He lived in a way that is a model of how we should live today, and his teaching has the extraordinary wisdom to guide us as we seek good solutions for the problems we face.

As I pondered this challenge to follow Jesus, I began to put my feelings and understanding in order and use them as a motivation to address why and how the church should make a more consistent effort to solve our severe problems. How might the values of Jesus guide us in caring for the earth? I soon discovered and was encouraged to learn that a great deal of wise and thoughtful work is already being done in addressing climate change and the deteriorating environment by religious organizations. In fact, it would be accurate to say that there is a global movement within the church and interfaith organizations, one motivated and informed by their sacred scripture, the Hebrew prophets, the vast flow of human thought and action within Hinduism, the teaching of Buddha, the life and teaching of

13. Unfortunately, there are also a number of sectarian groups claiming they are the "true church" but who are cultic, exclusive, and tribal; they are more a part of the problem than part of the solution.

Jesus, Muhammad's gift of Islam, and the profound thought of contemporary religious leaders. The Christian church and other religious organizations have a clear mandate to care for our earth home and make it more sensitive and more responsive to human need and, as far as possible, to make Mother Earth a healthy setting for all of life as we know it.[14]

This renewed awareness invited me to increase my knowledge about what is being done and then to consider how I might contribute. Being retired and no longer directly involved as an active member within the leadership systems of the church, I felt a tug to restudy the teaching of the great prophets of the Hebrew Bible and grasp in a renewed way how these visionary prophets, the ethical teaching of great religious teachers, and in particular the teaching of Jesus point us toward ways of caring for Mother Earth.[15]

Almost immediately I thought of the foundational teachings of the Hebrew Bible and turned to the parabolic description of creation in the first two chapters of Genesis. Within these brief words, there is as a profound theology of creation, understood as a wonderful blessing for which we are responsible. I went back through the wisdom literature in the Hebrew Bible and reread Ps 8: "When I look at your heavens, the work of your fingers, the moon and the stars that you have established; what are human beings that you are mindful of them, mortals that you care for them?" (vv. 3–4). I realized that the God of the cosmos cares for the human family and asks the religious community, in particular, with divine guidance, to share the divine love by caring for the welfare of the earth and making it a good and safe home for all of life.

As I read and reread passages of the Bible, reviewed much of the commentary on those passages, and explored the topic of caring for the earth in

14. The church has not always been responsible, but it has great potential to be a positive influence in the world. Neither have its members always been consistent in living responsibly, yet Jesus remains the one who embodied the values that we need to follow in this crisis moment in human history.

15. The literature is abundant. See two publications of the Presbyterian Church (U.S.A.), *The Book of Order* and *The Book of Confessions*, which contain several documents that outline ways for the Presbyterian Church to be a compassionate force in creating a more just world. The "Brief Statement of Faith," a relatively recent document (1983), says we "exploit neighbor and nature, and threaten death to the planet entrusted to our care. We deserve God's condemnation. Yet God acts with justice and mercy to redeem creation." I have also written in my book *The Spirituality of the World Religions* that these religious families must use their resources in a collaborative way to address the threat to our global home.

the literature of Hinduism, Buddhism, Islam, and other religious traditions, I sought to understand the teaching of visionary religious leaders who have spoken about our earth home. It was not hard to find general guidance. At the heart of the great prophets of the Hebrew Bible, the Christian church's teaching, and prophetic voices in contemporary religious thought, I heard the common call to understand the "big picture" description of the threat, to prepare myself to help care for our earth home, and then to live a life, as Jesus did, as an advocate for justice and peace and engage in actions of responsible love and compassion.

I was deeply moved by these remarkable insights, and they became a calling; that is, I heard the divine voice calling me to see clearly the needs of those who suffer, to be compassionate and understand how to help (to see), to prepare myself for responsible action through study and practical experience (to be), and then to engage in spreading the wings of love to care for the earth (to do). As I reviewed what it means to see, to be, and to do, I found myself reviewing the life and values of Jesus and saw him as the one to follow.

I began the intimidating task of using the teaching of the prophets of the Hebrew Bible, the life and teaching of Jesus, the wise teaching and counsel of the first Christians such as the apostle Paul, the Judeo-Christian tradition, and the profound insights of other religious traditions as guidance for my understanding of the threats to our home and how to help. I needed to prepare myself to make a contribution to healing Mother Earth and then to make a modest contribution to solve some of the problems that threaten her. I am also in the process of inviting others to join in this new gathering of people of concern. We won't totally remedy the climate change crisis, establish a peaceful world, overcome poverty and hunger, and reduce the several other threats to global health, but those of us who have become more enlightened, visionary, and compassionate can help.

Jesus was such a person, sensing a call from God to teach, heal, and proclaim the message of the reign of God. He went about his calling in a direct and straightforward way, visiting the small towns of Israel-Palestine for an extended period of nearly three years.[16] In time, he sensed the need to go to Jerusalem. He paused along the way in different villages and the town of Jericho before he entered Jerusalem. Jericho, an ancient city, was a place of modest importance and power.

16. It is not altogether clear how long Jesus remained in Galilee. Three years is the suggested time, although other scholars make a case for a shorter period.

He also took the time to stop on a hill in order to prepare for the climax of his vision. It was in this setting that he and his disciples reaffirmed their calling and experienced it in a vivid way. This vision is called the transfiguration, one in which there was clear guidance from the leaders in the history of Israel, reassuring Jesus that he was on the right track.

I am proposing that we now learn how to engage others as Jesus did, going where the people are present and their needs are pronounced, teaching, healing, and proclaiming the will and way of God. It was there that he said to his followers, "The light is with you a little longer, walk while you have the light, so that the darkness may not overtake you. If you walk in the darkness, you do not know where you are going. While you have the light, believe in the light, so that you may become children of the light" (John 12:35–36).[17]

Now is the time for us to walk in the light and join together to manage our current realities. To do so, we will need a common outlook, a frame of reference, and a mind and heart that will guide as we turn our attention to care for our threatened world. *Having the heart and mind of Jesus will help us go to the source of our problems, help us gain perspective on them, and point us to solutions.* His heart and mind, that is, his outlook and perspective,[18] have the following components:

17. The Greek word translated here as "walk" does mean to go further, beyond where one is in the present, which may be dangerous (darkness), but can lead to the light so one may see where they are going and engage in doing good. The first letter of Peter underlines the need to walk in the steps of Jesus: "For to this you have been called, because Christ also suffered for you, leaving an example, so that you should follow in his steps" (1 Pet 2:21).

18. I run the risk, as I speak of the "heart and mind of Jesus," of being presumptuous, knowing how complex his outlook may have been, how descriptions of who he was and how he lived are numerous and varied, and the multitude of ways he has been understood. It is difficult to discern who he was and how he lived even for the best scholars and teachers. Yet the in the last two hundred years or more, there has been a modest consensus among scholars that it is quite difficult to know with clarity who he was and what he taught. It is the case that more conservative clergy and laypeople really believe they do learn what they need to know about Jesus from reading the Gospels. There is a gap between the views of lay church workers and New Testament scholars about how one "goes back" into history, whether one should read and accept in a literal way the accounts in the Gospels or use the best methods of historical scholarship to be sure we are "truly getting back to the Jesus of history." I am saying that we can understand enough from the New Testament records, supplemented by excellent scholarship, to discern the outlook, point of view, and perspective of Jesus and be guided by it. It is possible, if done with care and diligence, to speak about his "mind and heart," his outlook, and his perspective on how we should live our lives.

1. First, he said that our lives should be filled with unconditional love: "If then there is any encouragement in Christ, any consolation from love, any sharing in the Spirit, any compassion and sympathy, make my joy complete: be of the same mind, having the same love, being in full accord and of one mind" (Phil 2:1–2). The apostle's brief introduction in this section of his letter to the Philippian Christians underlines that love is the foundation for the unity and mission of this new congregation. He says to them that if they want a life-giving church and a fulfilling life, then they should come together and have love as the core of their being, giving them unity in their common life and mission. The love about which the apostle Paul speaks is *agape* love, the love that reaches out to all people and accepts them in an unconditional way, even if they are not "lovely." It is the love for which we all long: to be accepted, embraced, and nurtured. It is a love that is compassionate, caring deeply about the suffering and the challenges of others.

2. Paul underlines that if this love is present, it means that our focus in life is not self-centered; it is not driven by selfish ambition or conceit, exclusively pursuing our own interests. Rather it is focused on the interests of others, caring deeply about the lives of others, their health, well-being, and their challenges.

3. The mind of Jesus was not self-centered, but humble and responsive to the will and way of God. Jesus, godly as he was, did not play his "divine card,"[19] "but emptied himself, taking the form of a slave, being born in human likeness. And being found in human form, he humbled himself and became obedient to the point of death—even death on the cross" (Phil 2:6–8).

4. God therefore exalted Jesus: "Therefore, God highly exalted him, and gave him the name that is above every name, so that at the name of Jesus every knee should bend, in heaven and on earth and under the earth, and every tongue confess that Jesus is Lord, to the glory of God" (Phil 2:9–11).

We get clarity from Paul in his description of the mind and heart of Jesus about what should be our attitude and spirit, our outlook, our heart and mind, as we respond to others and the world around us. He says clearly, referencing Jesus, "Let this same mind be in you" (Phil 2:5). As we go into

19. He was not some kind, human god who had unusual power, but a human being like we are, although with a deep commitment to do the will of God.

our troubled world, we need to follow Jesus, be filled with love and compassion, care deeply about peace and justice, and understand what it means to follow Jesus in helping to create a more just and humane world.

QUESTIONS FOR REFLECTION AND DISCUSSION

1. Does religion in general and the Christian faith in particular provide insight and wisdom that helps us assess our current social and political realities?
2. What are some of the ways that these insights speak directly to a particular concern in our time?
3. How would you describe the relevance of Jesus in your particular social setting, that is, where you live and where you work?
4. How has your mind changed over the last three or four years regarding your view about religious faith and its relevance in your life and the life of our country?
5. How did Jesus relate to the major governments in his context: Jewish authorities in his immediate setting, regionally with the Herod family, and nationally with the Roman occupation?

BOOKS TO CONSULT

1. Marcus J. Borg and N. T. Wright, *The Meaning of Jesus*
2. Hugo Echegaray, *The Practice of Jesus*
3. Bart D. Ehrman, *Jesus: Apocalyptic Prophet of the New Millennium*
4. Richard A. Horsley, *Jesus and the Politics of Roman Palestine*
5. Elaine Pagels, *Miracles and Wonder: The Historical Mystery of Jesus*

SECTION ONE

To See: Understanding the Mind and Heart of Jesus

Jesus said to him, "I am the way, and the truth, and the life."

—John 14:6

As I TALK WITH a range of people who cross my path in the normal activities of a given day, I discover a great many who are in good health and have a positive outlook on life. They are not just managing the challenges of a given day, but are also finding a good measure of gratification in their family life, fulfillment in the work they are doing, and anticipation for a good future. They feel positive and hopeful about what they have accomplished, the ways they have connected with others, and how they have been able to express in tangible ways an inner purpose and meaning in their day-to-day lives. They understand their responsibilities in a perilous world (see reality clearly), have the abilities and resources to help improve the life of others and especially those who suffer (are prepared to meet the challenges), and have the insight and knowledge to engage in work that contributes to the welfare of the human family and Mother Earth (do good work).

As we look at our own lives and the lives of those around us, we discover that there are different levels of motivation and abilities as we seek to engage in this meaningful life. There are many people who have found their way, feel gratified in their life work, and find life fulfilling and rewarding. There is an even larger group in the middle of the informed-uninformed scale who find that life is essentially positive, although the combination of external threatening forces and their limited internal capacity to cope make life a daily challenge. These people make it through the day, yet arrive at home in the evening feeling stressed, and perhaps use some form of "attitude adjustment." They still sense that life is good because the work is manageable; there is love in the family and the home is comfortable, although their jobs are stressful. Of course, there is still another group of people who arrive at home (or may not have a home) quite stressed, feeling that the day was filled with negative experiences and that they have not wisely managed the array of tasks and relationships in their lives. There is tension, frustration, and deep fear that the pathway they are on may not lead them to a good life. There is little understanding and comfort from wherever, whatever, and whoever they think of as being home. It is this last group that especially needs wise intervention and help.

As we have just one life to live, I am proposing that we follow a way of life that Jesus modeled and cultivate the outlook and perspective of Jesus; he is the model of doing good in the world, and his frame of reference as he went from place to place was motivated and empowered by the eternal values of truth, love, justice, and peace. Jesus modeled a way of life based on these values as he walked from Galilee to Gaza; he incarnated these values and proclaimed the transforming grace of God.[1] He realized his goals because he embodied the truths that he taught. He expressed deep love and practical guidance and help for all; he cared deeply about the need to face reality, to speak the truth, to respond with understanding and compassion, and to engage in creating a just society that leads to peace.

Again and again, he underlined that his followers should continue his work. Yet he was aware that it would not be easy for his followers to continue what he started. So, he carefully taught them by his example, his wisdom, and his vision, and then engaged in creating a new environment filled with love, justice, and peace. He told his followers about this vision and then illustrated that it is possible to be transformed by the loving grace of God, engage in spreading the love of God, and being active in creating a more just and humane society. His way of guiding his followers was to underline that one can be transformed by being open to and receiving the very presence of God; divine grace empowers one to be filled with truth

1. Jesus traveled to many different settings, although he stayed within the boundaries of present-day Israel-Palestine.

and love.[2] He often used the expression "kingdom of God" as a way to speak about having the full presence of God in one's life.[3] It was his way of inviting his followers to be open to and embrace the empowering grace of God in their lives and to let God reign. In his language and teaching, he encouraged all who heard his voice to sing: "Spirit of the living God, fall afresh on me."[4] He invited all who heard him to become part of God's family, to be transformed by God's grace, and then to have an outlook, a frame of reference, and a mind and heart that empowers one to be God's messenger of love.

In his time, as in ours, awareness about the nature of reality that surrounded them and love as compassionate care were noticeably absent in the lives of the people with whom he associated. What he saw and spoke about was the need to overcome ignorance, discontent, and passivity, and then to affirm and practice the true faith of the Jewish people. This was his mission. He taught that true faith was grounded in the belief that all humans need to open their hearts and minds and invite the full presence of God to dwell there. By doing this, one would then have a new outlook, be transformed, and have a foundational frame of reference rooted in truth and love. He urged them to seek the "kingdom" of God, that is, the reign of God in one's life.[5] To do so was to be transformed by the God of love and truth and be filled with God's presence. It was his way of inviting his listeners to live in a way that is open to the presence of God, having a life full of meaning and purpose and being a part of a community in which God reigns. In this new kingdom of God, one will follow the leading of God in the mission to address injustice, poverty, illness, and hunger. He said to all who heard him

2. See William Keepin's book *Belonging to God: Spirituality, Science and a Universal Path of Divine Love.*

3. The term "kingdom of God" has been interpreted in many ways, although behind these interpretations is the nation of the reign of God.

4. This is the title of a hymn written by American Presbyterian pastor by Daniel Iverson.

5. The word "kingdom" is somewhat problematic because it is masculine, and it may not fully point to the ruler's responsibility to create a just and humane setting for those who dwell in it. However, his intention was to speak in a way that his listeners could understand, and he used the metaphor of a ruling king to point to God's ruling power. Further, there is the difficulty of precisely understanding the meaning of "the kingdom of God," a concept that has been understood in a variety of ways. I have used the term to mean "reign of God," that is, to establish a peaceful and just society. Others have understood it in a more apocalyptic way, with God intervening and overthrowing resistance to the full reign of God in history.

that we should have a life based on faith in God, ultimate truth, and be filled with the divine presence (God is love), and then we will be empowered to "tune in" to God's will and way and live with the values of Jesus.

One will then have the capacity to begin to understand the complexity of truth and be guided by it. It gives one the capacity to see the vast range and depth of human suffering and then be motivated to express love in all those settings where it is absent. Following Jesus means that our outlook and frame of reference have been changed. We now understand that we have the responsibility to live in a truthful and loving way. As we have responsibilities in our context of life, our outlook—our mind and heart—are rooted in the divine, and the God of love and truth will empower us to see clearly, to follow the way of Jesus, and to act responsibly.

Behind this invitation to embrace this new way of life was the way Jesus, God's messenger, saw human suffering and affirmed the notion that our hearts and minds can be transformed as we invite God to be fully present in our lives. As he often spoke to them in Hebrew, he may have used the Hebrew words *nephesh*, *ruach*, and *leb*, which translate into English as an outlook and frame of reference, our core identity and way of understanding. They point to what we mean by our center, our heart and mind, our consciousness where the presence of God is felt and honored. It is to invite God to be the center of our identity, and from this center comes the profound experience of God's love and the motivation to follow the way of God in one's life. We follow the example of Jesus.[6]

It is where we receive the deep truth that is repeated and underlined by the apostle Paul as he urges the Philippian Christians to "let this same *mind* be in you that was in Christ Jesus" (Phil 2:5, emphasis added). As Paul uses the word "mind" in the Greek, he means that it is the central place in human experience where God enters our lives, where religious experiences and commitments have their root and then determine our behavior. He urges them to open their hearts and to receive what was at the heart of Jesus, his essential outlook, the way he understood reality and what motivated his actions. The apostle Paul, in his words to the Philippian Christians, is essentially saying, "Have this outlook that was the heart of the life and teaching of Jesus."

6. This counsel to follow Jesus may easily be criticized as naïve and a return to the model of the liberal Christianity of the early twentieth century. My answer, as one might expect, is "Yes, but . . . it was not wrong, but it may have underestimated the enormous power of evil and the multiple causes of suffering."

MAY I BE STRONG IN THE SPIRIT

Dear God, my prayer today is for your divine assistance to help me be

Strong in spirit,
Courageous in action,
Gentle of heart.
May I act in wisdom,
Conquer my fear and doubt,
Discover my own hidden gifts.
My desire, Lord, is to
Meet others with compassion,
Be a source of healing energies,
And face each day with hope and joy.

QUESTIONS FOR REFLECTION AND DISCUSSION

1. How would you describe your physical, mental, and spiritual condition? Good? Not so good? Needing guidance?
2. Do you have good personal and intimate relations that are life-giving, as in a good marriage, a healthy family, and trusted friendships? If not, what are you doing to cultivate them?
3. Do you find joy in and have a deep appreciation for the beauty in art and in nature? Is there a spiritual dimension for these feelings?
4. Do you have a reasonable standard of living and either satisfying work or the anticipation of satisfying work if you are still in the stage of preparation?
5. Do you have a religious or philosophical outlook that "puts things together" and fosters resilience in managing life?[7]

7. I am drawing upon Carl Jung's list of the "Five Pillars for the Good Life." Jung, *Modern Man*, 95–114.

BOOKS TO CONSULT

1. Thomas Berry, *The Sacred Universe: Earth, Spirituality, and Religion in the Twenty-First Century*
2. Denise and John Carmody, *Ways to the Center: An Introduction to World Religions*
3. Elaine Pagels, *Miracles and Wonder: The Historical Mystery of Jesus*
4. David Richo, *How to Be an Adult: A Handbook on Psychological and Spiritual Integration*
5. Richard Rohr, *Everything Belongs*

Chapter One

Learning the Dimensions of the Mind and Heart of Jesus in His Context

Enter through the narrow gate; for the gate is wide and the road is easy that leads to destruction, and there are many who take it. For the gate is narrow and the road is hard that leads to life, and there are few that find it.

—Matthew 7:13–14

The "gate is narrow and the road is hard" as we begin to understand and cultivate the foundational outlook of Jesus, one patterned on his life and teaching. As I explore the spirit and life of Jesus, I want to do so from a historical perspective, focusing on the life of Jesus as a first-century craftsman, and later a teacher, prophet, and healer in a premodern time. It is foreign culture for most of us, and to understand Jesus and his mission in depth is no small task!

In the area of Jesus studies over the past few centuries, one finds mountains of research and writing. It is a complex subject, and understanding requires that we enter into his setting, culture, and language. Yet even with these challenges, I still want to suggest that we can essentially get to first-century Israel-Palestine. Thankfully, marvelous and motivated scholars have done much of this work and made it available to us. There is, of course, diversity in this massive array of scholarship, yet there is also a modest consensus and a call for new research.

As we move to this broad understanding, I want first to underline a general agreement among scholars, teachers, and pastors who speak and write about the life of Jesus. It is that the body of this work may be classified as either the study of the "Jesus of history" or a study of the "Christ of faith." Both approaches are valuable to those with interest and especially to the church. Often, as the two approaches are integrated, it is possible to speak about a remarkable human being living in first-century Israel-Palestine who has a divine identity. It is to value the historical study and then to accept the church's affirmation that Jesus is Lord and Savior.[1]

This extraordinary quest of understanding may go in another direction, assuming that he was a human like us and the categories we use to speak about him are those that describe human identity and action. It is an attempt to follow Jesus as an exceptional teacher and prophet, yet fully human, and through his life and teaching we learn about how to live in a spiritual way.

I lean toward focusing on the Jesus of history in this writing because I want his life and teaching to be understood as coming from a historical person who lived in the first century and whose life and teaching can guide us; he was human as we are. As we study these statements, we discern that it has not been all that easy to make this distinction between the Jesus of history and the Christ of faith. I have both read and heard many of these slightly different views of Jesus. I will tend toward a focus on the first-century Jewish teacher who was fully human, although it will be difficult not to take into account the point of view that he was also in some sense divine; he belonged to God. It will make it somewhat easier for us to understand Jesus as a model for us when he is understood as sharing our humanity.[2] He, then, is one we can identify with and emulate, although those in the Christian church may also see him as the second person in the Trinity—Father, Son, and Holy Spirit whom we worship. I have now been a student of the life of Jesus for several decades. I now find myself returning to the study, and as I do, I continue to find a treasure beyond description.

1. A careful attempt to honor history and the church's belief is the four-volume work of John P. Meier, *A Marginal Jew: Rethinking the Historical Jesus.*

2. There are those, of course, who say that such a distinction is not wise and perhaps fails to describe Jesus in an accurate way. I have deep sympathy for this caution, and I will honor it as we attempt to find and understand the first-century Jewish person named Jesus. My goal at this point in the writing is to understand Jesus as human, not unlike who we are; if he is human as we are, we may be more able to fully identify with him and honor the goal of living as he did.

His life and teaching are profound and compelling, and for me, now more than ever, he is the model of life to emulate.[3]

JESUS AS OUR MODEL

Current mental health research occasionally uses the language of "inside-out" and "outside-in" to classify the ways we fail to mature and face the challenges of life in a healthy manner. The goal, of course, is to find a way of living and being educated that is fulfilling and provides a sense of accomplishment and inner peace.[4] Across the centuries, as thoughtful scholars and therapists have discussed and written about both good and not so good mental health, they have generally begun their analysis by saying the problems are either internal or external. If they are internal, there is a condition present in our current identity and values, part of the essential person that we are. Therefore, it is difficult for me to manage the demands and challenges in life. It is difficult for me to navigate my life in order to have a deep sense of finding a good and healthy way to live (inside-out). Or we may find that the stresses and strains in our environment and current way of life are overwhelming and need to be changed for us to find a healthy and peaceful life (outside-in).

The therapy, then, is getting help to either modify our internal makeup so that we can cope with the challenges of life, or to carefully face our external environment and explore how it might be changed so that we can manage our circumstances and flourish in our setting in life. We either

3. In the last couple of centuries, there have been those who say that Jesus is the model of life for us. Yet there has been another movement that does not reject that he is a great model so much as to suggest that we really can't get back to him using the best critical methods. Yes, we do need to be careful that we don't just bend history to help us create Jesus "in our image" while just paying partial respect to the critical historical method. More recently, not only in scholarship, but also in my heart and life, I have been converted to understanding Jesus as a model for life. My scholarship suggests it can be done, the perilous world that surrounds suggest that it is needed, and I have been reconverted to the conviction that we can know a great deal about Jesus. And, as I engage in the study of his life and teaching, I believe his life and teaching give us the best hope we have in our dangerous times. I am also aware that I am identifying what is now being called neoliberalism, a return to a movement that had great influence on scholarship and the church more than a hundred years ago, but perhaps now some of the dust has been removed.

4. See the book by Warren Kinghorn, *Wayfaring: A Christian Approach to Mental Health Care*, chapter 3, "From Inside Out to Outside In," 83–110.

endeavor to change our current internal way of managing in order to cope with life, or we change the harmful impact of our setting so that we find a healthy context in which to live. As Jesus traveled from city to town and to campsite, he came with the goal to change a setting in which people lived (outside in), and also to transform those whom he met (inside out). We now must learn how to place Jesus in the context of our goal to heal and move toward maturity. In what ways might he become our model, the one whom we follow?

HOLISTIC HEALTH

Not long after Jesus started his public ministry, as he and his disciples were in Galilee,

> a leper came to him begging him, and kneeling he said to him, "If you choose, you can make me clean." Moved with pity, Jesus stretch out his hand and touched him, and said to him, "I do choose. Be made clean!" Immediately the leprosy left him, and he was made clean. After sternly warning him, he sent him away at once, saying to him, "See that you say nothing to anyone; but go, show yourself to the priest, and offer for your cleansing what Moses commanded, as a testimony to them." (Mark 1:40–44)

In this brief story, we see Jesus healing the leper (inside out) and telling him to enter back into his normal life (outside in).[5] He was free from his disease and could return to a healthy pattern of life.

Competent scholars and therapists, drawing upon both the internal struggle and negative external factors, have suggested a variety of ways to understand mental health and how to achieve an advanced level of maturity, one filled with peace and purpose. One pattern, rooted in the teaching of mid–twentieth-century scholars and therapists, speaks of our mental health as subjective, emphasizing emotional well-being with the absence of negative emotion and having a good measure of positive feelings and attitudes. It is often spoken of as human flourishing with the presence of positive relationships, having a clear sense of purpose and meaning and

5. At the time of Jesus, the word "leper" was occasionally used as a general term for illness, not a reference to the disease that we now know as leprosy. Yet it was known as contagious, and so this person would have been isolated and needed approval from the priest to reenter normal life.

feeling gratified in and connected to the social context of one's life.[6] Human flourishing is defined as having positive emotion, engagement in meaningful activity (work), connecting in a constructive way with society, having authentic relationships, and feeling a sense of purpose and accomplishment. The leper's disease was healed, and, as far as we know, he returned to a normal life, had positive relationships, and found his place within his setting.

Drawing to some extent on the work of therapists and clinicians, another pattern for understanding health and maturity emerged, one that viewed human life as unfolding and moving through several stages. This view affirmed that the pattern of human development is to reach maturity at each stage of life and then move on to the tasks inherent in the next level of maturity. Growth toward maturity is a step-by-step hike, a stage-by-stage process. One significant contributor to this way of understanding human growth and development is Erik H. Erikson, who used the assumptions of developmental psychology and underlined the significant task of all people to shape and understand the process of forming their identity.[7] He places this developmental task of shaping one's identity in the context of the life cycle (the flow of life), identifying each stage of development and its essential task. He describes these several stages, each with the significant challenge of accomplishing the particular developmental growth goal of the stage. When the growth goal is achieved, the person is empowered to advance toward another level of development, moving toward becoming a healthy and mature adult. There are several stages:

1. Stage one is infancy, with the task of achieving the "mutuality of recognition"[8] between the child and the parents or caring adults. In this first stage of life, the infant either feels loved and accepted and therefore begins to trust the emerging identity, or not accepted and feels mistrust and moves toward autistic isolation. Growth toward healthy development comes with loving acceptance by our parents and the responsible adults near us. Healthy development may be blocked if there is excessive fear and rejection.

6. The work of Erik Erickson, Carl Rogers, and Abraham Maslow have provided many of the categories of this understanding. See Kinghorn, *Wayfaring*, 154–59.

7. Erikson, *Identity*. In this book, Erik Erickson suggests eight levels or stages.

8. Erikson, *Identity*, 96.

2. In early childhood there is the essential task of becoming and the will to stay on a healthy path leading to our best possible self. As the child develops, there is either a measure of self-certainty and comfort that comes with the acceptance of one's growth by the adults in one's life, or a measure of rejection by one's parents or caregivers and the rise of an uncomfortable self-consciousness that leads to shame and doubt.
3. As one moves toward adolescence, a very important level, there is either the healthy feeling of self-acceptance in the pattern of becoming or the sense of rejection by others in the circle of nearness that creates fear, guilt, and a poor self-image. One either feels positive because there is a measure of affirmation from others or discomfort because there is a level of neglect or rejection by others. Where there is rejection, the person has a fixation, controlled by guilt, and a deep feeling of being unacceptable without the resources to do something about it.
4. Early adulthood provides either a positive apprenticeship in adult life because of a fine education, life-giving relationships, and a good measure of accomplishments, or it may be a time where there is a work paralysis filled with the feelings of being inferior, a sense of being unable to manage the complexity of one's setting, and a fear of rejection in the family or school setting.
5. Adulthood, then, comes with a positive sense of one's identity or a negative sense that one is not acceptable. The result of rejection is the presence of a sense of futility and the lack of a positive role in life.
6. Adulthood continues to be positive, with a clear identity, or negative, with the confusion about roles in life and one's capacity to measure up to expectations.
7. Across the years, then, there is a healthy sense of self with the capacity for intimacy and personal value, or the loss of self-worth and the inability to authentically connect with others, leading to isolation.
8. Life continues with the capacity to flourish with self-acceptance, clear values, and accomplishment or the sense of stagnation, with a poor self-image and a confusion about responsibilities, beliefs, and values.

STAGES OF FAITH

In the last third of the twentieth century, Dr. James Fowler, a scholar in developmental psychology and religion, incorporated these categories of Erik Erikson and the thought of several other development psychologists and applied them to spiritual formation. He used this broad structure of stages of development not only as a way to understand how to become a mature adult, but also as a way to help and inform those seeking a deeper and more mature faith. The categories crossed over to help us understand how it is that we mature in our faith and spiritual formation.[9]

In *Stages of Faith*, Dr. Fowler introduced his broad theme of spiritual formation by first identifying faith as more than just a casual affirmation of a list of religious beliefs; he maintains that faith should be understood as a profound orientation in life. As there are stages of growth and development in becoming a mature person, so there are stages of faith and a process of cultivating a mature, informed, and engaged faith.[10] In *Becoming Adult, Becoming Christian*, he integrates the stages of faith with the stages of human development.

Dr. Fowler describes the context in which there can be healthy or unhealthy development and underlines initially that American society has gone through a sort crisis of vocation, focusing almost exclusively on our society's pattern of just getting a job that pays well.[11] The risk in this orientation is that the deeper understanding of one's identity and values may be set aside. If this happens, one feels confused and unfulfilled in the work setting. As far as possible, the vocation of the person should be an easy blend with the formation of a congruent identity, clear values, and a sense of self-worth. Humans thrive when they understand their day-to-day work as a calling, which easily integrates with their development, values, and identity.

He speaks about the need to cultivate an internal voice and an awareness that informs us about how we have a constructive role to fill in our society.[12] It is possible and very important for us to have a vocation that takes into account our identity and values, contributes to meeting the needs of people, and in some ways may contribute to creating a healthy and just

9. See his two books, *Stages of Faith: The Psychology of Human Development and the Quest for Meaning* and *Becoming Adult, Becoming Christian: Adult Development and Christian Faith.*

10. Fowler, *Stages of Faith*, 127–211.

11. Fowler, *Becoming Adult*, 48–75.

12. Fowler, *Becoming Adult*, 52–70.

social order. This sense of vocation has the capacity to give integrative order, meaning, and purpose to one's life. It will help us find and have an important role to fill in our social context and guide us through our adult years.

This sense of identity and role in life need not necessarily be defined in religious language. Yet when it is, we sense that we are becoming what God intended for us; there is a pattern of development that enables and empowers us to do God's will as we make a positive contribution to our setting in life. In short, we bring our mature faith to the many dimensions of our lives and especially in our relationships and the work we do. We have a sense of vocation and see our work as contributing to the well-being of those we serve. We "do good for God." In this larger frame of reference, we sense that our vocation or divine calling is expressed in the work we do in that it helps to create a more just and humane society; we contribute to the betterment of society.

How is it that we reach the point of having a mature, informed, and engaged faith that guides us across the years and in our many roles? Ideally, in the best of conditions, we generally move through several stages of faith, with each stage having its own worth as a necessary phase in our growth. It is acceptable, then, to be in process and at any point in these stages of faith.[13] We are on the way, understanding that life is a process of becoming.

In our very early life, there is *infancy and undifferentiated faith*,[14] an innocence that trusts that all is well because of the loving care of parents or those in a parental role. God's love is like that of my loving parent. Yes, there might be mistrust because of neglect of or harm to the child. When that occurs, the child will have difficulty in sensing that a loving God might be present. Ideally, the child is loved and accepted, reflecting the counsel of Jesus that we should have faith like that of a child who fully trusts the goodness of God: God is like my loving parents. Or it may be that the conditions of childhood have been negative, with neglect or even harm causing the child not to trust the statements about God's love. As we move from childhood innocence and growth toward adulthood, it is likely that the sense of how we were cared for will shape how we feel about God and influence the early development of faith.

13. Not everyone, of course, will be able to move through all these stages of faith. We do get bogged down in our personal growth and not infrequently may join a church or faith community that is not healthy; there may be a cultic and tribal character to the community of faith, one that is exclusive and judgmental.

14. Fowler, *Stages of Faith*, 119–21.

Stage 1 is *intuitive and projected faith.*[15] It is based on our capacity to trust what we experience and are told by loving parents and our community of faith. "God loves me, this I know," and I can rest and be content with this reassurance; I know what it feels like. With lack of care and neglect, the child may find it difficult to understand and accept that "God loves me."

Stage 2 is *mythic-literal faith,*[16] which develops, usually in late childhood, by the way faith is expressed to us in the stories we are told about God's unconditional love, a love that surrounds and protects us and is illustrated with tangible and authentic stories. These stories and illustrations may have a trace of symbols or metaphors that point to a much deeper faith understanding, but the meaning of these symbols and pointers are more fully learned at a later stage in life. We begin in our growth and development by accepting and trusting the tangible words and actions of loving parents and what and how they tell us about God's love. It is literal truth expressed in story form rather than an abstract statement pointing to a deeper truth. It is acceptable to be at this point in one's development, knowing that there will be a more advanced understanding of the faith journey as we mature. On occasion, some adults do remain at this mythic-literal stage in their faith development.

Stage 3 is *synthetic-conventional faith.*[17] At this stage, there is an acceptance of the Bible's teaching and the stories and accounts of Jesus, or comparable stories if the family has a different faith orientation. In these early school years, often there is the presence of the tangible stories about the love of God, often with references to biblical stories where love is a central theme. The child sings, "This I know, for the Bible tells me so." Our churches, synagogues, and temples teach that God created the world and made it so that life can be good and filled with trust and joy. There is no need, at this stage, for an emphasis on understanding the twenty-four-hour days of creation as historical epochs and the creation story as a subtle and sophisticated parable. The child can grasp that God sent Jesus (or a prophet and teacher) to save and guide us, but there is little need to explain the causes of evil and suffering or, in the Christian context, to use the framework of the death of Jesus in the context of substitutionary atonement. The ethical guidance is to follow the examples of those who have lived exemplary lives, using them as examples of how we should live from day to day. The

15. Fowler, *Stages of Faith*, 122–34.

16. Fowler, *Stages of Faith*, 135–50.

17. Fowler, *Stages of Faith*, 151–73.

notion of evil and disobedience are present, and there is the need to speak about them in the context of faith; the child will be able to understand them in terms of their age and experience. The wise parent will place them in the context of the ethical teaching of Jesus and forgiveness and acceptance by God. The emphasis in the Christian context is to lift up the ethical teaching of Jesus as guidance for being kind to others. Many adults remain at this level in their faith journey; the typical Christian church is filled with people at this stage of faith. It is a good place to be for the church and its people, although people at this level may find it difficult to deal with the intellectual challenges aimed at religious belief. The challenges may be either ignored or denied, often using a passage from the Bible to give them reassurance.

Stage 4 is *individuative-reflective faith*,[18] a stage of faith that takes into account that faith does change and mature, and that most people of faith enter the process of making faith their own, applying it to the context of their life and seeing it as much-needed wisdom about how to navigate life in a rapidly changing and perilous time in history. Christians of nearly every stripe understand that there is a process of growing in their faith. They understand that God is present in their lives and will empower them to cope and mature.

Those in this stage of faith acknowledge and generally understand that the Bible comes to us as a pre-scientific document written prior to a critical historical understanding of these ancient events. It is a collection of documents in which there is great wisdom and guidance, and we learn from the Bible (and the church or temple) how to discern God's love and guidance. At this stage, there is a tendency for most people to reflect on faith and discover how the Bible and the teaching of the church, synagogue, or temple may guide their lives and suggest ways of understanding the world around them. The Bible contains an invaluable history and the guidance of God. At this stage, often with some questioning about the meaning of faith, people seek to understand faith in the context of history, science, and the wider world. It is a good place for many pilgrims of faith, although at this stage there is the need to have comfort with some unanswered questions. One does not cease to be Christian or spiritual because there are questions; in fact, searching and finding answers to these questions advances one's commitment to and understanding of faith.

18. Fowler, *Stages of Faith*, 174–83. Dr. Fowler prefers the word "individuative," although the word "individual" might work just as well.

Stage 5 is *conjunctive faith*,[19] a stage that is not all that easy to define because of its many dimensions and expressions. In general, it is that stage in which one feels comfortable to ask questions about the many aspects of one's faith and how we might frame the foundational components of faith that make it more compatible with a contemporary worldview. It is usually a time of expanding one's orientation and exploring how faith fits within the larger framework of human knowledge. It is still possible to affirm that our religion can be the great teacher of our lives. The Bible may be viewed as a remarkable piece of literature, containing profound insight and ethical guidance. We understand it best by reading it from a critical-historical perspective, enhancing our understanding. It as an invaluable source of wisdom especially for Jews and Christians. Jesus was one of several great teachers of the human family, and we learn from him. We advance our religious views and spiritual life as we learn from the Hebrew Bible, the teaching of Jesus in the New Testament, and many other rich sources of religious and spiritual guidance.

Stage 6 is *universalizing faith*,[20] a position that is open to profound ideas and practical wisdom from many cultures and traditions. At this stage, one also accepts the best of scientific research and the most profound expression of how to live wisely and well. The person at this stage is willing to say that the Christian, and indeed all people on a faith journey, can and should be open to many faith traditions, the best thinking and scholarship in religious thought, and the finest reflections on how to lead a life filled with wisdom and profound ethical guidance. One remains open to the process of learning, understanding, and maturing.

It is possible, as one is exposed the best resources for discerning the meaning of faith, to move from the earlier stages of faith to the more advanced stages of faith. But it is important to note that all of these stages are appropriate in the life journey, and one should not discount the earlier stages of faith. We are in process, moving through life, and our advancement to the later stages of faith may occur, often by being intentional about seeking a deeper understanding of the faith journey. But judgments, such as saying that the earlier stages are inadequate, even in some sense wrong or unhealthy, is unwise. To say it as a person of faith, I believe that God honors both our present stage and new stages as they emerge. It may be that our circumstances lead us there. God honors our movement through the

19. Fowler, *Stages of Faith*, 184–98.

20. Fowler, *Stages of Faith*, 199–210.

stages of faith, as we reflect, pay attention to wise guidance, and cultivate the capacity to discover a deeper reality.

As Jesus entered into his ministry with his disciples, a leper came to him and asked for help. Jesus responded by healing his disease and urging him to weave his way back into a normal life. It was an act of healing the whole person. The disease was cured, there was support for him in the community of faith, and he was acknowledged as a faithful person on the way toward maturity and fulfillment. In a sense, we go to Jesus like the leper and ask for help. We seek his teaching about human need, the presence of unconditional love and grace, the call to practice compassion and seek justice, and the answers he gives in his life and teaching; and we seek to follow him.

QUESTIONS FOR REFLECTION AND DISCUSSION

1. What is the appropriate way to nuance and wisely affirm our statements of faith in an informed way, especially if there are differences in what we have been taught to believe and what is widely accepted and understood as the truth because of careful scholarship?
2. What are some differences between what is often called simple faith and informed faith? Is it possible to integrate classical statements of faith with New Testament scholarship? How do "simple" and "informed" come together in our faith?
3. How would you describe yourself: 1) a true believer, 2) a person of faith who has some honest doubts about how faith is understood and taught, 3) a person who is in process and growing toward a more informed faith, 4) one who is trying to integrate faith with a knowledge-based understanding of the contemporary world of knowledge, or 5) one who does not feel the need to be a person of faith but desires inner peace on life's journey?
4. Using the categories of James Fowler describing those with faith, where would you place yourself? Where are you in your faith journey?
   - Infancy and undifferentiated faith
   - Intuitive and projected faith
   - Mythic-literal faith
   - Synthetic-conventional faith

- Individuative-reflective faith
- Conjunctive faith (the position of holding two orientations at the same time)
- Universalizing faith

5. What would you most like to do in the future in reference to the life of faith?

   - Stay pretty much as is with no deep needs to change.
   - Become more spiritual in the sense of both deep internal peace and a commitment to "do good" and seek justice in my setting.
   - Become better informed about my faith, sensing that I am growing in true faith.
   - Become better informed about how I might integrate my faith with contemporary knowledge.
   - Find ways to reach out to people and help them heal their bodies and find life-giving ways to enter into relationships and the social order.

Books to Consult

1. Erik H. Erikson, *Identity: Youth and Crisis*
2. James W. Fowler, *Stages of Faith: The Psychology of Human Development and the Quest for Meaning*
3. Warren Kinghorn, *Wayfaring: A Christian Approach to Mental Health Care*
4. Thomas Merton, *Contemplation in a World of Action*
5. Ronald Rolheiser, *Sacred Fire: A Vision for a Deeper Human and Christian Maturity*

Chapter Two

Enhancing Our Capacity to Have the Mind and Heart of Jesus in Our Context

By the tender mercy of our God, the dawn from on high will break upon us, to give light to those who sit in darkness and in the shadow of death, to guide our feet into the way of peace.

—Luke 1:78–79

Again, he entered synagogue, and a man was there who had a withered hand. They watched him to see whether he would cure him on the Sabbath, so they might accuse him. And he said to the man with a withered hand, "Come forward." Then he said to them, "Is it lawful to do good or to do harm on the sabbath, to save life or to kill?" But they were silent. He looked around at them with anger; he was grieved at the hardness of heart and said to the man, "Stretch out your hand." He stretched it out, and his hand was restored. The Pharisees went out and immediately conspired with the Herodians against him, how to destroy him.

—Mark 3:1–6

PATTERNS OF HEALING, LOVING, AND TRANSFORMATION

Great thinkers and healers across history, from Buddha to Plato, from Jesus to Muhammad, and from Einstein to the Dalai Lama,[1] have

1. And hundreds more.

addressed the problems of human health and wholeness and have either leaned slightly toward the need to heal the sick soul (inside-out) or eliminate a harmful environment (outside-in) as part of their frame of reference and outlook on life. I expect, if we could get them all in the same room to talk about the good and healthy life, they all would acknowledge that in some sense both our internal make-up and our environmental setting contribute to our health and happiness and also to our illness and discontent. Their understanding of their growth and healing strategy would be influenced by their outlook on reality, their frame of reference, and their personal experience. These dimensions have shaped their heart and mind.

We want to understand how to move within our faith outlook toward comprehensive health and peace of mind by exploring both perspectives, the inside-out and outside-in, that is, how both our internal make-up and our environmental context can contribute to our healing and health and help us find our way. Jesus, when healing the man with the withered hand, did heal his hand (inside-out), but had to deal with an external threat (outside-in).

We have maintained that as we journey and continue to find the best way to flourish in this confusing and perilous world, we do need to understand our world and our environment (to *see* clearly and find a spiritual pathway that has integrity). We need to be diligent in our quest to understand, aware that it is the truth that sets us free and has power to guide us to our true home of peace and purpose. We need to discern the truth and invite the healing power of truth into our lives; and we do that if we have the right frame of reference, an outlook on life and reality that grasps the truth and embraces it. We are maintaining that such an outlook should be comparable to the one that was present in Jesus, empowering him to embrace the truth and heal the sick and misinformed.

If we seek to find our home within a religious context, sensing that Jesus got it right, it is important for us to put the words "true" or "truly" in front of the words "spiritual" and "spirituality." There is some risk in our quest for a spiritual center (having the heart and mind of Jesus) because it is explained and taught to us by those who are shaped by their culture, language, experience, and place in history. It is possible, regardless of our sincerity and starting point, to understand ourselves and our world in immature and less than accurate ways. There will be a trace of this across the years.

If this tendency is generally present across the years of our lives, then we need a way to see it, reduce its influence as far as possible, and seek to "have this mind in you that was in Christ Jesus." Even as we are developing and growing from childhood, good parents will seek to help their children to have an outlook in life based on understanding the truth and loving one's family and friends. As far as we are able, we need to seek an authentic and well-grounded foundation based on a true understanding of reality. If such a foundation is elusive and beyond our scope of understanding, we need to know that our teachers are committed to such a foundational outlook, that our outlook can change, and that it can be guided and developed within our community of faith.

In addition, it is wise to take into account that not all religious traditions and spiritual pathways are as committed to the truth as they should be, nor do they always ensure that their claim to have the truth is supported by a rigorous method to ascertain the truth. Across my many decades of reading statements of faith and observing religious practices, I have discovered that our religious beliefs are inevitably partial products of our culture and historical traditions. Those who teach us are usually wise, and our trust in these teachers is usually at a high level as it should be. Only occasionally is there the acknowledgment by the representatives of these faith traditions that what they teach has the dimension of their limited reflections on the place of the divine in human experience. More frequently, there is the sense that what they are teaching is not an approximation of the truth, limited by language, culture, and history. For example, those with limited exposure to the vast array of the many profound spiritual traditions and without a clear understanding of how to discern the truth may understand their religious thought and practice as "the Truth." And it is for them, yet their view will be somewhat limited by their failure to understand that nearly all religious views are limited by the context and culture out of which they have come. As these descriptions and ideas are passed down to succeeding generations, they will contain the traces of the perspectives of their time and place in history and their culture. Seldom do these teachers fully understand and acknowledge that their religious outlook is approximate. Yet even with some limitations, there are still many settings that enable a pilgrim to experience and understand the religious message. It can be one that has authenticity and maturity, even if the hard work of historical study has not been completed. Yet we as wise adults do know that this inevitable limitation will be present, and then we do our teaching with care, having as our foundation the "same mind . . . that was in Christ Jesus" (Phil 2:5).

It is important to note that our ideas and practices, rooted in a cultural understanding, do have a kind of "experiential truth," that is, they become true *for me* in the sense of helping me cope and embrace a spiritual outlook that empowers me to grow, mature, and manage life where I am. We may not always be totally accurate and congruent in our interpretation of the life and teaching of the founders of our faith or sufficiently subtle in our understanding to accurately describe how the faith tradition has developed and fits in a contemporary setting. But the message of encountering the divine gets through to us as we learn from those who teach. We get a good start and begin to flourish, although it is a continuing process, one that lasts a lifetime.

It is also the case that there will be aspects of the process of spiritual growth that only a few will understand and experience. Not infrequently, it may be the theological foundation that may not be viewed as being as important as the experience, and so it not introduced. Or it may be that the process of spiritual growth and understanding should factor in historical and scientific information, giving one's faith a more solid and relevant connection. For example, few will fully understand how to integrate their faith with cosmic evolution or quantum theory or how to interpret the founding documents using a rigorous historical-critical methodology.[2] Yet these limitations do not block a personal encounter and ongoing connection with the divine, understood in different ways.

Since the subject matter in this journey is so important, these explanations and descriptions of religion and the divine sometimes take the form of being absolute truth in order to bring a sense of security to believers in a world filled with danger, uncertainty, and competing points of view. Our understanding of faith then runs the risk of being an expression of "fundamentalism" or "absolute truth" because we need it (truth) rather than because the way the message is proclaimed merits the description of being called the truth. We are wise when we accept that there is much to learn and that there may be some challenges to understanding the historical accounts and metaphysical foundations of the faith journey. Our views will generally contain an understanding rooted in one historical era, one culture, and one language. Yet, we can walk with authentic faith even if the descriptions and statements of belief are not totally integrated when judged by the methods and outcomes of contemporary scholarship.

2. See, for example, *Quantum Body: The New Science of Living a Longer, Healthier, More Vital Life* by Deepak Chopra.

For example, as we turn to the Bible for guidance in the Judeo-Christian traditions, we read and are invited to understand the story of Joshua. We note that God was on the side of Joshua, who fought the battle of Jericho because the "people of God" needed to advance to their promised land. On the other hand, if I had been in Jericho, I would have called the invaders aggressors, not spiritual leaders. It is difficult for me to believe that God is on the side of those who kill others and take their land, although I can affirm that the pathway of the children of God to a better land was the right direction, even as I can say that God was the Creator, although the creation took more than six days.

Religious thought and historical descriptions need to be as completely true as possible, and even then, it is appropriate to question, restate, and understand that what is being said may have felt truthful to those who initially expressed it, but less so in another time in history or another culture and language. It is acceptable on occasion to call into question an interpretation that is deeply rooted in a cultural prejudice and may even be self-serving. It is not a violation of faith to understand the historical context of a faith statement. To see clearly requires that we be diligent about being truthful. God is light, and in God, there is no darkness. These observations underline that we need a mature and well-grounded faith.

It is also very important to be diligent about how it is that we are able to heal and grow toward maturity (to *be* transformed and *be* healthy). No one of us is perfect, and there will always be a measure of human frailty. Our capacity to love, help, and heal others does not always depend on us being perfect. Though limited in our capacities, we can still help others. Yet, as we are led by God to lend a hand to those in need, the extent to which we will be able to accomplish these goals does depend in part on our capacity and skill to truly help others.

In short, there will be the risk of imposing our dated views and of using inappropriate methods that may impose our limited outlook on those we are trying to help. In fact, our view may be rooted in our needs and limited understanding. So, we need to diligently prepare ourselves to *be* a good counselor or a good doctor or a good religious leader in order to move from our limited frame of reference to our goal of being healthy, informed, and mature in our service. Who and what we are will make a huge difference in how well we heal and help.

As I teach, I do so in a better way when I am prepared, that is, if I have been educated and trained to do the work that is in front of me. We then find mature and gratifying ways to live and fulfill our calling *to be* the person who is able to make a positive contribution. We want to be well trained and mature in order to help those in our circle of nearness. We are *see-be-doers*, and the middle part of our name is "be," that is, a person who is prepared and mature, who can contribute to the common good.

Our third word is "do," that is, we use our understanding (we see clearly) and our development as mature people (our transformed presence and abilities) to do the work before us. It is *see* and *be*, and we then come to *do* and find that our work must be done in a world that is not only deeply troubled and perilous but is also changing rapidly. Therefore, it is easy for us who are called to serve to be dated and out of touch. We venture out to do good, but find that we must navigate through a dangerous swamp in order to arrive on a safer shore. We may barely recognize our surroundings. Almost daily, we come to a new shore with a dock we do not recognize and boats we have never seen. To change the metaphor, we enter a dense forest with different foliage and without clear and safe trails. We may be greeted by a person we do not recognize, who speaks a different language, and who wonders why we ask questions about a setting that no longer exists. We wonder if we have misread the map, but are reassured that we are at our right destination. Yet we may still feel ill-prepared to find who and what we are seeking. To say it still another way, we are asked to dance on a moving stage with new background music, different props, and rearranged furniture. Yet we do not give up, but enter into the risks of loving others in tangible ways. We are "doers." True love and the expression of compassion become our calling.

CHECKS AND BALANCES: GETTING IT RIGHT AS WE FOLLOW JESUS

One of the risks of teaching and affirming a religion and inviting a response of faith, not always mentioned, is that there are dimensions of the life of faith that are filled with danger. We are told that religion (usually a particular one) can solve our problems, heal us, and give us peace of mind. We are not always taught that a faith response to religion, while inviting a whole-souled commitment that leads to joy and peace, may also lead us in a false direction and cause suffering. A religious commitment, of course, can be very positive and should lead to a good and healthy life; yet when taken seriously, it has a powerful influence on us. So, we need to make sure that our religious beliefs and practices, as far as possible, are rooted in truth, contain wisdom, and are nurturing, giving us the resources to cope and manage what comes our way in our challenged lives.

We are asked then to do some profound study and reflection on how our faith may shape our self-understanding, our sense of purpose and meaning, and the values that guide us. We are wise to be aware of how our religious beliefs and commitments have and will impact our lives. Has our faith added a life-giving dimension in our journey, enhancing positive growth and providing a healthy pathway to peace and purpose? Or has it blocked our growth and invited us into a narrow and sectarian way of life, one that slows down our journey to health and maturity and leads into a tribal, cultic, and exclusive orientation? As far as possible, we want a religious outlook to emancipate us from misguided beliefs and dangerous practices, one that invites us to a faith that is credible, understands complexity, leads to maturity, and prepares us to engage in loving service.

There is an abundance of information about the different religions of the human family.[3] We can usually get the information we need in the community in which we live. It may come from those who live near us and even family members. Our libraries and bookstores are full of resources that speak about the beliefs and values of a religious orientation. As we engage in this inquiry, we may want a summary of the positive features of a religious-spiritual way of life; it will help us to be discerning. The summary of the positive features of a religious outlook would include:

1. Ethical guidance: understanding what values guide us to the good life, one filled with wise choices that enable us to live in a moral and responsible way.
2. Meaning in life: having a sense of our purpose, such as loving others and helping them grow into maturity, and a keen sense of responsibility.
3. Sense of belonging: having a healthy community full of joy, support, and loving relationships.
4. Security: having an environment that is safe in day-to-day responsibilities, across the years of one's life, and in facing the end of life.
5. Ways of coping: guidance on how to manage threat, pain, disappointment, illness, and broken relationships with faith and courage.

3. I have taught courses in the field of world religions and have been introduced to their complexity and vast assortment of details.

There are an equal number of risks when we commit to a religious point of view or outlook. A religious outlook may contain the following negative dimensions:

1. Narrow and limiting: preventing us from experiencing many of the joys of life and unnecessarily limiting both our range of thought and behavior.
2. Tribal: giving us the sense that we are right and have all the truth and others are wrong and need to stay on their side of the river.
3. Cultic: teaching the we alone have the right beliefs and secret practices.
4. Judgmental: since we have the true beliefs and the correct patterns of life, others must be wrong and should be called into account.
5. Exclusive: since we have the true beliefs and the right ways to live, we need to stay away from others who might influence us in harmful ways. They are inferior to us.

Over time and exposure to others, we move toward finding and developing a mature faith orientation. It is characterized by the way the following patterns of belief and practice become an integral part of day-to-day life:

1. We begin to experience the promised sense of deep peace and meaning in life. We continue to grow into this deep meaning and find a purposeful way to live wisely and well as we move through life.
2. We continue to grow in our understanding of our setting, our natural habitat, our region, and our country, the undergirding values of these domains, and the ways they may offer a good life for us and our family. We begin to understand the relationship of our faith to these different domains and learn the place and nature of our role in our setting, our country, and even in the context of our world.
3. We continue to move toward healthy behavior that is mature and sensitive to others, and find our role in helping those in need and how we may contribute to the formation of a just and humane society.
4. We find ourselves in a community, and we work to make it one that gives its members a good quality education, safe and comfortable housing, and an array of healthy ways to make a living, find deep and gratifying relationships, and make a positive contribution to the region.

5. In short, we sense that we have chosen the right vocation and community, and that we are in the right place doing the right things at the right time.

QUESTIONS FOR DISCUSSION AND REFLECTION

1. Do you occasionally find within yourself with a strong desire to help and/or heal another person? What is it that you would like to accomplish?
2. What are the cultural norms that guide you in your desire to help a person?
3. Have you ever done a good deed and then be criticized for entering into a situation that is "none of your business"?
4. Where do you place yourself in the stages of development and maturity?
5. Where are you in the stages of faith categories?

BOOKS TO CONSULT

1. James W. Fowler, *Becoming Adult, Becoming Christian: Adult Development and Christian Faith*
2. Henri J. M. Nouwen, *Life of the Beloved: Spiritual Living in a Secular World*
3. Hans Küng, *On Being a Christian*
4. Richard Rohr, *The Universal Christ: How a Forgotten Reality Can Change Everything We See, Hope for, and Believe*
5. Roger Walsh, *Essential Spirituality: The 7 Central Practices to Awaken Heart and Mind*

Chapter Three

Expressing the Mind and Heart of Jesus in the Present

He entered Jericho and was passing through it. A man was there named Zacchaeus; he was a chief tax collector and was rich. He was trying to see who Jesus was, but on account of the crowd he could not, because he was short in stature. So, he ran on ahead and climbed a sycamore tree to see him because he was going to pass that way. When Jesus came to the place, he looked up and said to him, "Zacchaeus, hurry and come down; for I must stay at your house today." So, he hurried down and was happy to welcome him. All who saw it began to grumble and said, "He has gone to be the guest of one who is a sinner." Zacchaeus stood there and said to the Lord, "Look, half of my possessions, Lord, I will give to the poor; and if I have defrauded anyone of anything, I will pay back four times as much." Then Jesus said to him, "Today salvation has come to this house, because he too is a son of Abraham. For the Son of Man came to seek and save the lost."

—Luke 19:1–10

MODELS OF MATURITY AND FAITHFUL SERVICE

As we look back across the history of the people of faith, we discover that there are several of models of mature faith, ones that have been expressed in a variety of ways due to the historical setting, its culture, its language, and its challenges. I will mention five broad categories but know that there is almost a unique expression of faith in each person's life. Often these differences are thought of as vocations, a "calling" that gives one an identity, maturity, and mission in life.

A study of the New Testament suggests that there are different callings, that is, different ways that we are guided by the Spirit of God about how to express our faith, use the gifts and talents we have, and understand the nature of our service given our abilities and circumstances. The New Testament does suggest that we have been given talents that are enhanced by and expressed in a calling. A naturally caring person, for example, may be called to a ministry of healing.

We are able to see how we might serve, using our talents and special gifts, as we read about the life and ministry of Jesus. Consistently, he demonstrated love for individuals in need and was concerned with healing and nurturing the whole person, healing their body, challenging their mind, and nurturing their soul. He empowered them to live wisely and well. He also expressed a deep concern for just and humane society, one in which all people would be treated fairly and with compassion. We, too, may assist in a neighbor's physical healing, find good ways to enhance their faith, and help them find a humane and just context in which to live. We may offer a way for others to have good physical health, have an informed faith, feel forgiven and loved, and ensure they are in a safe and peaceful context. Our goal is to find a way to help all those who come our way in all aspects of their lives.

The Gospels contain stories of the ways that Jesus demonstrated a concern for many people in very different circumstances. The Gospel of Matthew has one story that illustrates the concern of Jesus for the total well-being of a suffering and needy person: "And just then some people were carrying a paralyzed man lying on a bed. When Jesus saw their faith, he said to the paralytic, 'Take heart, son; your sins are forgiven'" (Matt 9:2). Jesus said, "Stand up, take your bed and go to your home" (Matt 9:6). The people were amazed that Jesus addressed the relationship with God, the healing of the body, and the need to "go home" to a safe and secure location. The sick person was on the pathway to being healed and finding peace and purpose in life. The authorities were more concerned about what could be done by Jesus, and the crowds were amazed. The authorities may have thought Jesus had "crossed the line" in terms of divine capability and an appropriate role.

As we study the life and teaching of Jesus and see the way he walks a spiritual pathway, we often find that there are some similarities between the calling of God that Jesus received and the one that comes to us as well. Yes, there are deep differences, of course, given who he was and the setting in which he lived. Yet Jesus, too, had to take care of his body, likely prayed that God would nurture his soul, and had studied his faith tradition. He had lots of good answers to hard questions! His life is a model of how God heals us, enlightens our minds, and nurtures our souls. With his life as our example, we learn that God receives our honest expression of faith and commitment. We are transformed, and then invited (sent) into the world to live by faith in our calling to love and serve. To grasp this point and deepen our understanding, I want to illustrate how God calls and empowers us by looking the lives and service of several gifted and saintly people, each of whom responded to the invitation of God to live into a vocation that was rooted in their dedication to the will and way of God. They addressed profound needs, utilizing their background and gifts, and were empowered to serve with faith and dedication. These people not only helped individuals, but modeled theological understanding of service in keeping with the needs of the people in their time and location. In many cases, they informed and changed part of the Christian understanding of God's will and way in the world. We may find our way by looking at those who have gone before us and found a mature spiritual way to live and serve.

THE LIFE OF SERVICE

All of us who live with faith and a dedication to God will be called to the life of service, generally to a setting in which we have an appropriate background, an adequate level of maturity, and the gifts that match the needs of people who will be served. One example, widely known beyond its context, is the selfless service of Mother Teresa. A profound area of need existed within the country of India and especially so in the city of Calcutta; in fact, the need was nearly overwhelming. There was poverty, sickness, and little hope that the situation might improve with a change in government intervention and support. It was a setting without the benefit of already existing and well-supported social programs or the likelihood of a much-needed change in the social structures. Individuals, especially those who were ill or elderly, did not have any hope or promise of getting medical help, a safe place to live, an introduction to a life of meaning and purpose, or an opportunity to move up the ladder of income and pursue the advancement of a career.

It was into this setting that a young woman, Mother Teresa (1919–97) as she became known, volunteered to help and was sent by the church to a place with profound need. She was from Skopje, Macedonia, had Albanian parents, and was not specifically trained or experienced in the work to which she was called. She was a very young nurse and sensed the presence of God in her life, although her experience and background would not suggest that she take on such a profound challenge.

As a young person, she felt called by God to serve the poorest of the poor and was appointed to serve by Missionaries of Charity (MC) in 1946. She was sent to Calcutta, a large city in India, one that had suffered from the partition in India with the Muslim population becoming East and West Pakistan. These conditions, caused in part by political changes, created profound challenges in Calcutta, many the product of profound poverty.

Mother Teresa took as her guide a literal reading Matt 25:35–36: "For I was hungry and you gave me food, I was thirsty and you gave me something to drink, I was a stranger and you visited me, I was naked and you gave me clothing, I was sick and you took care of me, I was in prison and you visited me."

When asked why she chose to serve in such a setting, she replied,

> My secret is quite simple. I pray and through my prayer I become one in love with Christ, and see that praying to him is to love him, and that means to fulfill his words. Remember the words of St. Matthew's Gospel:
>
> "I was hungry and you gave me no food,
> I was thirsty and you gave me no drink,
> I was a stranger and you did not welcome me,
> Naked and you did not clothe me,
> Sick and in prison and you did not visit me."[1]

She wrote, "My poor ones in the world's slum are like the suffering Christ. In them God's Son lives and dies, and through them God shows me his true face. Prayer for me means becoming twenty-four hours a day at one with the will of Jesus to live for him, through him, and with him."[2]

Over the last several years, as her story has been told, the vast majority of people have honored her (a Nobel Peace Prize) and praised her work. Yet

1. Teresa, *Life in the Spirit*, 1.
2. Teresa, *Life in the Spirit*, 1.

there has been another voice that has pointed out that she was also quite human, occasionally not wise in her administrative work, and not always gentle and kind with those who occasionally questioned her authority. She even acknowledged that there were times when she felt overwhelmed, made some mistakes of judgment, and became impatient with those in deep need. She wrote, "If I ever become a Saint—I will surely be one of 'darkness.' I will continually be absent from heaven—to the light of those in darkness on earth."[3] Yet even with this bow to modesty and limitation, there are few who would not acknowledge the profound and sacrificial character of her life. She in many ways epitomizes the life of service. We might summarize the life of service as having the following qualities:

1. Sacrificial service: With care for the service to the needy more than care for one's salary, prestige, family life, comfort, and location. Occasionally, our service may be in very difficult settings. And not all of them will be in poverty; there may also be difficulty in serving in an upper-middle-class setting where the values of money, prestige, and power prevail.
2. Limited salary: The location of the work of dedicated service may be determined by the needs in a particular location rather than from a setting where one has comfort, security, and beautiful surroundings. We are called to serve where there is need.
3. Levels of discomfort: To be committed to a life of service may mean being placed in a setting among the poor and the needy, having housing that lacks beauty and ease of living, and not being close to friends and family.
4. Demanding tasks: The tasks of a given day may not always be enriching and gratifying, though necessary in order to maintain and advance the mission of the church.
5. Limited retirement income: As one ages, there may not always be the promise of a comfortable and fulfilling retirement with easy choices of how and where to live, how to use one's time, and opportunities to enjoy the luxuries of wealth.

Toward the end of her life, Mother Teresa was recognized and honored for her work, graciously accepted the recognition she received, yet continued her commitment to a life of service. It became a context of praise

3. Kolodiejchuk, *Mother Teresa*, v.

and admiration for her work, and she used the recognition as a means to advance the work to serve the poor, well beyond the setting of Calcutta.

THE LIFE OF ETHICAL INTEGRITY

There are many people who have felt called to a life of service to help people in need. Generally, the work to which they are called is understood as needing the service of a person with integrity and the skills and experience deemed as requirements for serving in a particular setting. In most cases, it is having the education and experience needed in the work of the new calling. Generally, the person considering the appointment has values that match the values inherent in the context of the work. In most cases there is what is thought of as a "good match" between the candidate and the open position. In addition, there is accuracy in describing the position and a resume that accurately reflects the applying person's qualifications. I want to describe a context that was complicated, as often happens, one in which the job description (or need in this case) and the resume of the applicant were not an immediately obvious or a perfect match.

This was the experience of Dietrich Bonhoeffer, a young German theologian, one doing advanced graduate study in theology at Union Seminary in New York during the time when there was a change in the leadership of the German government.[4] The new government was led by Adolf Hitler, who wanted to expand his country to an empire and was moving the country toward conditions that would lead to the start of the Second World War.

Dietrich Bonhoeffer, born in 1906, grew up in a middle-class home in Breslau, Germany, had supportive parents, an excellent education, and every opportunity to be successful in life. What was not calculated by his family as they looked into his future in his early development was the rise of Adolph Hitler. It became a major factor shaping life in Germany and would profoundly influence Dietrich and his life following his university education. As a graduate student at Union Theological Seminary in New York, Dietrich had the opportunity to review the current theological views

4. There are several good resources for the study of Bonhoeffer's background, his theological outlook, and the unfolding of his life: the collection of his thought and writing, *Letters and Papers from Prison*; his own writing, such as *Ethics*; fine biographies, such as *Bonhoeffer: Pastor, Martyr, Prophet, Spy* by Eric Metaxas; and even a pictorial album, *The Steps of Bonhoeffer* by J. Martin Bailey and Douglas Gilbert. A short summary is difficult.

of the Christian church, had some questions and reservations about them, and leaned toward a more revolutionary faith, one committed to justice and peace. Hearing about the problematic situation in Germany, he decided to leave New York and a very promising career and return home to resist the Hitler regime.

On his return to Germany, because of the danger of the Hitler movement, he continued his reflections on the nature and role of the church and met often in hidden locations with colleagues who had similar views. A small fellowship was begun, current national issues were discussed, and these young men cultivated a profound commitment to intervene on behalf of their nation and its people, especially the Jewish community. They were profoundly opposed to Hitler. Dietrich wrote in July of 1944 about the need of the church to take some responsibility: true Christian commitment requires that Christians "are summoned to share in God's sufferings at the hands of a godless world. One must therefore live in the godless world, without attempting to gloss over or explain the ungodliness in some religious way or other. One must live a 'secular' life, and thereby share in God's suffering."[5] For Dietrich, the dedicated Christian could not ignore the horrendous presence and practices of Hitler and remain in the safety of graduate study in New York.

He was committed to this understanding of being Christian in the midst of tragic events and human suffering. In response, he continued to meet with a few other Christians, formed a small "underground" church, and began to speak openly about the need to form an active resistance to Hitler and his policies.

What became so significant to this group was the reality that any effort to stop Hitler would mean a possible resort to violence, understood by them as being forbidden by Christian teaching. In time, in reference to the extermination of the Jewish people, the group knew that bold action was required. Bonhoeffer would say, as the situation got worse, that those who do not resist the extermination of Jewish people are not worthy to share their history and be nurtured by their psalms. A plan to assassinate Hitler emerged in their small group and was carried out, filled as it was with profound complexity, both as an ethical choice and as a realistic goal, to resist the evil of Hitler's policy.

It failed, Dietrich was imprisoned, and much to the good of the prison camp, he became an informal chaplain to all who suffered in prison with

5. Bonhoeffer, *Letters and Papers*, 361.

him. It was in this prison where he wrote much of the material that is in the *Letters and Papers from Prison.* In time, his turn came for execution, and somewhat ironically, it was carried out just before the American soldiers reached the prison and freed all the prisoners.

We have much to learn from this deep and profound commitment to the truth and love of God by Dietrich Bonhoeffer. Many books have been written on this complex question of how to choose when the only choices have elements of actions to which one is opposed by deep conviction. For example:

1. There are times when there is so much evil and suffering that we may be asked to use a form of violence in our effort to stop a greater evil.
2. The church, as it is true to the teaching of Jesus, cannot hide behind the call to love others, retreat from resistance to evil, and sing sentimental hymns while brothers and sisters are being executed.
3. "Silence in the face of evil is itself evil. God will not hold us guiltless. Not to speak is to speak. Not to act is to act."[6]
4. Evil may come in many disguises, not always in bold public settings, and evil just below the surface may be as harmful to the spirit as poison gas is to the body.
5. There may be times when standing up for love and justice, even if it causes some conflict and perhaps suffering, is necessary. "Death is the supreme festival on the road to freedom."[7]

THE LIFE OF COMPREHENSIVE INCLUSION

There are many ways of "putting faith together," some focusing on a specific concern that captures the values and needs of an era. For example, in the latter part of twentieth century, there was the profound need for social justice (liberation theology), and the concern to ensure that women are treating equally in all aspects of life. They must be included in the leadership of the church and the formation of the church's belief and practice (feminist theology). There was the need to restate the faith in light of great social

6. A quote from Dietrich Bonhoeffer on the cover of Eric Metaxas's book *Bonhoeffer: Pastor, Martyr, Prophet, Spy.*

7. Bonhoeffer, quoted in Bailey and Gilbert, *Steps of Bonhoeffer*, 114–15.

change (political theology), and the need to be sure that the world of nature is included in the reflection (creation spirituality).[8]

In addition to these extremely valuable focused contributions, there have also been those who have tried, in the spirit of Augustine or Thomas Aquinas, to reinterpret the theology of the Christian faith in more inclusive categories that frame the Christian faith in its totality, with a focus on how it speaks to and fits within a historical era such as the modern or postmodern era. Again, there are many voices and choices, and I want to briefly mention two of them that sought to frame the Christian faith in a way that speaks to what one might call the modern era, the twentieth century, in quite different ways.[9]

There are many extraordinary theologians who felt the need for the church to frame its theology in the context of the deep changes that occurred in the nineteenth and twentieth centuries. It was vitally important to ensure the church's beliefs and practices addressed contemporary needs, modern thought, and a changing world.[10] I want briefly to look at two theologians, each one representing an alternative to the theological understanding that was not fully in touch with what was then called "the modern world."

I turn to two extraordinary theologians, one seeking to preserve the heart and essence of the church's theology while fully accepting and endorsing a modern rather than a premodern outlook (Karl Barth), and another one who maintained the need to make a bolder jump and transform the understanding of faith in the context of modern assumptions about science and, indeed, nearly all of contemporary life (Paul Tillich). Karl Barth (1886–1968), with many fine colleagues (e.g., Emil Brunner and, more recently, Jürgen Moltmann), was integral to the formation that is called neo-orthodoxy. From a Swiss (Basel) Reformed perspective, Barth, while engaging in important international conversations, devoted his time to writing what he considered to be a much-needed direction in Christian theology, namely a return to classic Christian theology with careful attention to the rise of modern thought and especially the critical historical study of the New Testament.

8. See Simpson, *Modern Christian Theology*, 368–68.

9. We will speak as well about theologies that move beyond "modern" to "postmodern."

10. As I speak of these, I am aware that they, too, sound partially out of date in that the world in now postmodern in so many ways.

He wrote a commentary on the Book of Romans (1919) that became a kind of symbolic start to a theological outlook that was central to the church in the twentieth century. Gradually, as he continued to write and was joined by many other fine scholars, a new movement called neo-orthodoxy emerged. It was affirmed by many as a way to retain a classic Christian understanding, while carefully responding to the need to acknowledge that the church's theology must intersect with contemporary thought and incorporate the finest current biblical scholarship.

Of course, there were some more conservative evangelicals that wanted to preserve the belief in an infallible and inerrant Bible and resisted neo-orthodoxy, while the more liberal and progressive side of the church thought that Barth had not gone far enough in the integrative task of finding common ground between a biblical perspective and contemporary thought.[11]

It would be hard to overstate Barth's influence, one that he shared with many colleagues such as Reinhold Niebuhr in the United States and even Rudolf Bultmann in Germany, who preserved a Christian outlook with a much more radical assessment of New Testament thought.

There were others who rose to the challenge of integrating classic biblical and theological thought with modern thought, and one extraordinary example is the work of Paul Tillich (1886–1965). It would not be altogether accurate to classify Paul Tillich as neo-orthodox, in that his effort at the integration of Christian thought with modern thought was less an effort to preserve classical Christian thought and more an effort to understand the Christian faith within the categories of modern philosophy with a particular emphasis on the issues raised in existentialism. His thought began with the givens of human experience and moved to the quest of the human need to find meaning. Tillich taught that God was and is the way to find meaning, but that the term "God" must be understood as the ground of being, not a man who lived in Israel-Palestine a long time ago. The heart of the Christian faith is the expression of God as that foundational ground of truth and understanding. As we find and embrace this living God, we do so with a new understanding of Being itself; new Being is made manifest in Jesus Christ.[12]

11. Karl Barth's many-volumed study of Christian theology, entitled *Church Dogmatics*, is one of the great classics of Christian thought, and one might hope that he is talking with Augustine and Aquinas in heaven. See, for example, *Church Dogmatics*, 2/2: *The Doctrine of God*.

12. Tillich's thought needs chapters to be understood. His small work *Dynamics of*

BIBLICAL FAITH AS THE GUIDE TO SOCIAL JUSTICE

Still another slight shift in the church's understanding of its beliefs and practices was present in the life and thought of Martin Luther King Jr. While Martin Luther King's life work was not primarily being a theologian, he did find within the Bible and the church's theology a profound expression of the need for justice in the social realities of humankind. As he experienced and observed the harsh realities of injustice, he pondered the ways that the biblical stories and the lives of its central characters, Moses and Jesus, addressed the need to challenge injustice. He reflected on the ways that he and his family were treated unjustly in their setting in Atlanta, Georgia. He then began to study how these two great champions of faith, Moses and Jesus, challenged the injustice of their time. It was Moses who led the resistance to the pharaoh of Egypt and said "Let my people go" (Exod 5:1) and then led the Jewish people across the water and underdeveloped land to the rightful home in Palestine. It was Jesus who challenged the Jewish system of government and the Roman power of his time, and he both articulated and personally expressed in tangible ways that God offers a life of freedom and love.

Martin Luther King Jr. took these grand examples of faith as foundational and used them as models to challenge the governmental systems and laws that were unjust in his time. He called upon the church to have integrity with its universal mission to create a just and human social order. He was particularly concerned about injustice in the Southeast of the United States, but in time, he addressed the need in the whole American system; unjust laws were embodied in the legal system and the way of life in the United States. His work and that of his many colleagues, were fundamental to the radical shift away from deep-rooted prejudice against African Americans and many other minorities.

In many ways, it was the story of the people of God, those who followed Moses and those who followed Jesus, that provided the model and inspiration for profound change to the legal systems and, indeed, challenged the assumptions of hurtful prejudice that caused so many people to suffer. It was the understanding of religious thought and action that made the difference, and for many, these social changes gave millions of people a new of understanding their faith and a better life.

Faith is good place to start, and his *Systematic Theology* in three volumes is a full expression of Tillich's theology, although a demanding read.

THE MOVE TOWARD INTEGRATION AND INTERFAITH UNDERSTANDING

As we seek to find the best ways to "put faith together," we do have these wonderful models from which to learn and, on occasion, to choose from as a pathway of faith for us. There is one more that I would like to mention, in part because it has a dimension that is common to all of the choices: that of integration. As we learn from and follow the deep truths and insights of biblical faith, we do engage in a process of integrating the biblical record (or the founding documents and the teaching of founders) with our contemporary understanding of the world, one driven in part by reason, our knowledge of science, and our current ways of understanding the world. There are many ways that we learn and know.

Often intentionally and carefully, although at times more informally, we do these two tasks as we sustain our faith: 1) we integrate it with what we know from years of learning, exposure to modern life, and our patterns of putting life together, and 2) we are likely to be in conversation with those of other faith traditions that engage in many of the same tasks, often with profound knowledge and exceptional wisdom. I want to offer a quick word, then, about this learning and the movement to engage in interfaith understanding.

The first is that we are often asked by our experience to integrate our faith with a scientific understanding of the world. One major pattern of understanding in our time is using the scientific method and discerning the discoveries of science. As we turn to the Bible, we cultivate a hermeneutical method that enables us to interpret the story of creation in the book of Genesis in light of our scientific understanding of the early formation of the planet. We may, for example, seek to explain the account of the creation of the world taking place in six days by exploring how the major eras of the formation of the cosmos might fit into this beautiful and profound parable. We know that science is the best teacher about the age of the created world and how it was formed, yet find wisdom in the ancient story in Genesis that makes the account profoundly personal.

I want to call attention to the work of French Catholic priest Pierre Teilhard de Chardin (1881–1955), who was a scientist and did some very creative work in integrating his faith with his scientific background. He was assigned to serve the church in China, and part of his service, in addition to the ministries of the church, was to continue to engage in scientific research about the origins of human beings. He was faithful in his calling, although, somewhat ironically, the church was not always ready to accept his views. His early and best-known book, *The Phenomenon of Man*, was a book that the church placed on "the dangerous list." It traced the surging and continuing evolution of the world from the primal stuff of the universe, through life, to consciousness and humankind. He continued his research, writing on various dimensions of this theme and exploring the many ways that evolution explains and informs our current state. Included among his many books are *The Future of Man*, *Man's Place in Nature*, *The Vision of the Past*, and *The Hymn of the Universe*. In *The Hymn of the Universe*, he speaks of the evolution of all that exists and invites us to understand the marvel of the created cosmos. For him, it led to the worship of the Creator and called him to serve the world in love. It is a hymn we need to sing as we find our way and live responsibly in our evolving world and universe.[13]

As those who understand that God's love is universal, we often ask how it is that we as Christians relate in love and respect for those in other faith traditions who also teach a way of life devoted to God. Books have been and are being written on this topic; it is complex and calls for our best thinking and deepest spiritual devotion. There are differences among the religions! We do need to be wise about how we best serve the will and way of God in these linkages with others who put their faith in different patterns from our own. I want to suggest—in a paragraph or two, not a book—how we might reach across boundaries and embrace others with a different outlook.

For starters, we reach out to those from other faith traditions with a good measure of understanding and compassion. We are careful about our assumptions and our criticism, in part because we may not fully understand and in part because we are called to the life of unconditional love. So, with careful and sincere listening and with deep empathy and respect, we begin the task to understand and connect. As we do, we will generally find that we have a great deal in common. We discover that we are all influenced by what we have been exposed to and taught within a particular language and culture, and that we will be in the presence of others who may have

13. A very gifted and creative scientist and religious person, Ilia Delio, has given her life to continuing the work of Teilhard, believing that the human family must find its way into the future by understanding the overarching reality of evolution, collaborating with its laws and systems. Her books include *The Unbearable Wholeness of Being: God, Evolution, and the Power of Love* and *The Emergent Christ: Exploring the Meaning of Catholic in an Evolutionary Universe.*

heard the voice of truth and wisdom in a different language and culture. We honor the sincerity of the beliefs and practices.

I have been influenced and taught by a multitude of wise and dear people from other religions, although two from the Buddhist tradition who have shared their understanding of the ethical life in writing have been especially enriching. As I read their work, I sensed there was a great deal of similarity in their ethical values, although some differences in the precise way to describe their faith. We turn first to the writing of the Dalai Lama and discover that his values are very similar to those taught in the teaching of Jesus. The Dalai Lama's book *Toward a True Kinship of Faiths: How the World's Religions Can Come Together* offers a welcoming gesture to others, with a marvelous understanding of both the differences between religions and also the presence of common beliefs and practices. With a compassionate heart for all those who need loving empathy, he accepts those with a different history and religious faith and asserts that we have so much in common as we care for all people and especially those who suffer. He and Jesus would have a lot in common in that he asserts that our task is to help and heal others, not judge them. It is the need for this universal love that unites us. Jesus loves the Roman soldier and the Palestinian woman at the well who gave him a drink of water. The Dalai Lama would have loved them as well.

Another teacher in the Buddhist tradition, recently passed away, is Thich Nhat Hanh, who taught universal love as the way to find a connection with those from a different religious orientation. This Buddhist monk was forced to leave his homeland in Viet Nam because of the war and settled in the south of France in a monastery. His teaching is very similar to that of Jesus who taught (and lived) that unconditional love and empathy for all is the foundational ethic of all of the great world religions. His marvelous writing invites all humans to come to listen and learn.[14]

There are many ways of leading the spiritual life and serving the will and way of God. We turn now to giving attention to our own personal backgrounds and how these patterns and ways may point us to a pattern of spirituality that is ideal for us.

14. His small book *Living Buddha, Living Christ* introduces the ways that humans can join in love and create a more caring and just world. An American Buddhist, Jack Kornfield, has taught and written with the same spirit. His book *A Path with Heart: A Guide Through the Perils and Promises of Spiritual Life* extends the hand of loving acceptance.

QUESTIONS FOR REFLECTION AND DISCUSSION

1. How would you describe your faith orientation?
2. Does it fit into any of the five types or schools of faith we described?
3. What other "schools" and patterns of faith have you studied, learned from by experience, or had an interest in?
4. What are the healthy (or unhealthy) aspects of your faith orientation?
5. Are there some aspects of your faith orientation you might want to modify or change?
6. What are some of the best ways to integrate your faith with contemporary life and thought? For example, how does it fit within a scientific understanding of nature, or a social science orientation toward the "good life"?
7. How does your faith enable you to better understand the politics of your country? Does the teaching of the Christian faith on love and justice give you some hope?

BOOKS TO CONSULT

Karl Barth, *The Doctrine of God* (book 2, volume 2 of *Church Dogmatics*)[15]
Dietrich Bonhoeffer, *Letters and Papers from Prison*
Martin Luther King Jr., *A Call to Conscience*
Brian Kolodiejchuk, ed., *Mother Teresa: Come Be My Light: The Private Writings of the Saint of Calcutta*
Pierre Teilhard de Chardin, *The Phenomenon of Man*

15. Karl Barth has written a number of books, and I have selected one from his great series, *Church Dogmatics*, in that it addresses a foundational concern of Christian theology: God.

SECTION TWO

To Be: Embracing the Mind and Heart of Jesus with Faith, Integrity, and Compassion

Again, Jesus spoke to them, saying, "I am the light of the world. Whoever follows me will never walk in darkness but will have the light of life."

—John 12:1

WALKING WAS A COMMON way of moving from one location to another in the time of Jesus. There were animals to ride for those unable to do the longer walks in order to take care of one's responsibilities and to visit family and friends. In most cases, the trails and roads, if not marked, were still relatively easy to follow. It was the way people moved from one location to another, and nearly every adult and even children had a sense of where to find the right trail or road in order to reach the desired location. But there were some problems, especially if one needed to travel in the darkness of the night. Not all manner of activities and conversations among families, friends, and business acquaintances occurred in the daylight hours. Many of these activities needed to be addressed after the sun had gone down, and people had to find their way in relative darkness. A form of using torches was available, yet even they had a time limit. Inevitably, there were times when one could get lost, or at least take the wrong trail and have to backtrack. Darkness was an integral part of the lives of those who lived prior to electricity. Getting lost or at least missing a trail and being late was not uncommon. There was a different sense of timing with friends and family, a slower pace, and the occurrence of getting lost if one was not familiar with the trail system. It was not unlike the contemporary experience of the hiker in the wilderness who wisely stops the hike as the sun goes down.

It was not uncommon to use the metaphor of getting lost in the darkness to describe a frustrating experience of being late for an appointment because one missed a turn or had to backtrack and wait for the sun to come up. From time to time, Jesus would draw upon this kind of experience and illustrate how easy it was to "get lost" in life when there is darkness (lack of knowledge and little information about direction). It was not uncommon for there to be frustration and confusion in darkness, and he on occasion would talk about his message as the light of life, overcoming a spiritual and psychological darkness. His listeners would have had the internal sense of having lost direction and the challenge of overcoming the frustration in not being able to reach a goal or even to manage life wisely and well. He spoke about being and having the light of the world. He taught that it was possible to gain insight into one's confusion about life, how to move from this darkness to have light, and then to become "insightful," that is, grasping the nature of a problem that caused pain and misdirection and then discovering a great truth and "insight" that frees one from lostness and moves them to the point in which they are able to see again. He taught that it was possible to get on the right trail that would take them to their spiritual home, overcoming the darkness.

Again and again, Jesus comes alongside a person who has lost his or her way, feels a high degree of frustration, and doesn't know how to find a good way through the psychological and spiritual wilderness. Our next section in this unfolding story will explore the life and teaching of Jesus as providing light, insight, and wisdom in order to find the best way to move out of the darkness and have "the light of life" (John 8:12). This process is to move out of the darkness into light, and then be motivated and empowered to find direction and meaning in life. It is "to be" in the best sense of having found one's identity and reason for living. It is "to be" rather than to live with worry and frustration. He speaks about the great existential insight that true living is to have deep gratification in being who we are; there is deep peace because one has discovered his or her identity and meaning in life. It is to go with Abraham from suicide to vibrant living, from frustration to flourishing.

ACTIVITY FOR REFLECTION AND DISCUSSION

Areas of Challenge

Write one sentence or even just a word that captures your anxiety level in reference to the challenges in your life.[1]

1. This is adapted from an Anxiety Awareness Questionnaire. I am unaware of whom I should credit in the use of the questionnaire. I have a practice of saving helpful handouts from conferences I have attended over a sixty-year period. It was in one of my files, and I am grateful to the person who carefully prepared the questions. I owe them lunch!

Chapter Four

Having the Faith to Bring the Mind and Heart of Jesus into the Context of One's Life

But strive for the greater gifts. And I will show you a more excellent way. . . . And now faith, hope, and love abide, these three; and the greatest of these is love.

—1 Corinthians 12:31, 13:13

THE BAPTISM BY JOHN

We have maintained that the journey through life is not always easy; in fact, we generally have to walk on trails that are dangerous and confusing. As we plan for this journey, we often reflect on the purpose of our journey, the challenges we will face, and the values that will guide us as we walk. There was a time in the life of Jesus when he decided to change his vocation from that of a carpenter to that of teacher, prophet, and healer. We do not have a lot of information about that interval in the life of Jesus between the time he traveled as a boy with his parents to Jerusalem and the time of his baptism in the Jordan River by his cousin John, but we can imagine that there were some risks as he grew from a boy to an adult. His father was likely a good teacher and his mother an extraordinary model of maturity. The best of our New Testament historians suggest that he may have worked with his father in construction as he matured, perhaps repairing and even making boats for those who fished in the Sea of Galilee. A bit later, likely after his father's passing, he may have served as a carpenter near a new city that was being built by Romans not far from Nazareth, his home in Galilee.[1]

1. We do not have sufficient historical records to trace these early years in detail, and

We pick up the story with his decision to travel south to the place where his cousin, John the Baptist, was baptizing people in the Jordan River and inviting them to seek forgiveness and rededicate their lives to their Jewish faith. As the cousins talked, Jesus said he was ready to be baptized in order to identify with their people, but John was reluctant to baptize Jesus, saying, "I need to be baptized by you, and why do you come to me?" He recognized the extraordinary character and presence of his cousin Jesus. Yet Jesus answered him: "Let it be so now; for it is proper for us in this way to fulfill all righteousness" (Matt 3:14–15). John felt some discomfort about baptizing Jesus in that he knew how faithful Jesus had been to the teaching of their common faith, and John's baptism was primarily for those who felt guilty about not fully living up to the expectations of their faith. But Jesus felt the need to "fulfill all righteousness," that is, to make sure he had met all the demands of the Law and that others observing him would recognize his faithfulness. He could then, with a clear conscience and good reputation, begin his public ministry, having fulfilled all the expectations of one who would dedicate his or her life to ministry as it was understood in that context.

Yet Jesus, while sensing full acceptance by God in the baptism, still felt a need to continue to prepare himself for his public ministry. There were many dimensions to his preparation for the role God had given him. Following his baptism, he traveled to a rural area, called by the biblical author a "wilderness" (Luke 3:4, 4:2). As have many, I have been to the location called by Jesus a wilderness. The wilderness was not a mountain region with a vast forest, but a desert region, dry and hot in the summer months and with limited access to food and water. One might wonder why Jesus, after his baptism, would still think there was a next step in his preparation for his life calling. In short, we might assume that he wanted to be sure he would be ready to face the challenges he anticipated as a teacher and prophet, one who would face many challenges, not the least of which would be some reinterpretation of the current teaching and practices of the religious life in the Judaism of his time.

---

we rely on the small clues we have in our records, and then project a possible path for his life until he becomes a public figure, following his baptism by his cousin John in the Jordan River. The Gospel of Matthew (2:13–18) includes a story of the family escaping to Egypt during the time when Herod was killing infants because he was afraid that one of them might grow up and displace him. The city that the Romans were building as Jesus was an adult is Sepphoris, not far from Nazareth.

THE TEMPTATIONS IN THE WILDERNESS

I find myself identifying with Jesus in his decision to go on a retreat in the wilderness and to prepare himself for his life calling. Yes, he had been taught about the life of faith by his dedicated parents, and for the most part, we assume he followed the prescribed ethical norms and religious practices of his Jewish faith. He could have easily returned to Nazareth and begun his public ministry without the retreat, yet the records indicate that he felt a profound sense of vocation, a calling to proclaim the good news of the kingdom of God. He understood the kingdom of God as the way God reigns in one's life and in one's place or region. He wanted to be ready for this difficult, demanding, and profound calling to be a voice for God's will and way.

As we read the account of this time in the life of Jesus, we learn that he felt called by God to invite people to a more dedicated spiritual way of life.[2] He knew it would be a demanding responsibility, one requiring deep dedication, an awareness that there would be resistance on the part of his listeners, and even objections to his type of ministry by the religious establishment. Jesus sensed that a retreat in the wilderness would deepen his dedication, give him courage, and provide wisdom as he fulfilled his calling as a teacher, prophet, and healer.

The story provides a very insightful description of his time in the wilderness. It was one filled with many temptations to give up on his calling. As a sort of summary of these days of dedication and what he experienced, we have an account that describes three of the great temptations of life that, if yielded to, would make him less than trustworthy in his calling to ministry. The author of Matthew's Gospel suggests that there is one fundamental and necessary domain of life that has within it the potential to cause one to turn away from one's deepest values. It is the temptation to abuse our need for physical gratification and comfort, going beyond that which adequately supports our physical well-being. Jesus, as one often does in such a retreat, fasts as a way of focusing on the need for obedience and courage to gain the strength to resist the physical temptations of life. In the account mentioned in Matthew's Gospel, Jesus has been fasting, and he was especially

2. I am aware that the records we have of Jesus are somewhat limited and have the influence of being written well after Jesus lived; there was the risk on the part of the author(s) to insert what they thought about this period of time and the early public life of Jesus. We trust their account because they had access those who were eyewitnesses, people who were trustworthy, not primarily because they were trained historians.

susceptible to the need for food and water in a desert region. Matthew records this experience of Jesus by saying,

> The tempter came and said to him, "If you are the Son of God, command these stones to become loaves of bread." But he answered, "It is written, 'One does not live by bread alone but by every word that comes from the mouth of God.'" (Matt 4:3–4)

This temptation had two elements of threat. One was to give up the dedication of fasting as a way to prepare himself to be the true expression and messenger of the will and way of God. Jesus knew that to be what he was called to be would require deep dedication and discipline, traits that cultivate the attitude and spirit necessary to his calling. He also appears to know in this kind of situation that temptation often comes to us in relatively innocent ways; that is, it is easy to say that it is all right to eat if you are hungry. The tempter says to Jesus, "If you are the Son of God, command these stones to become loaves of bread." Jesus, in his decision-making, could have said, "I can still be dedicated to God if I give up the commitments of my retreat in the wilderness. Does it really matter if I break the fast? And meeting my physical needs is acceptable by God; after all, I have to do it to stay alive. I do have some special power and perhaps could turn stones to bread." Yet he says to the tempter, "One does not live by bread alone but by every word that comes from the mouth of God." He will not be lured away by those temptations that appear on the surface to be innocent and natural.

In the second temptation, after resisting the need for food and the misuse of his God-given vocation, Jesus is invited, perhaps in his imagination, to go to the holy city of Jerusalem and be on the pinnacle of the temple. There, the evil one says, "If you are the Son of God, throw yourself down, for it is written, 'He will command his angels, concerning you,' and 'On their hands they will bear you up so that you will not dash your foot against a stone'" (Matt 4:5–6). If you really believe in God's love, jump off a tall building and God will save you. Jesus replies, "Again, it is written, 'Do not put the Lord God to the test'" (4:7). Jesus replies, essentially, "I work for God; God does not work for me. I will do what God says."

And there is third temptation, in which Jesus is taken to a high place and looks at all kingdoms of the world and their splendor, and he is told that it could all be his if he worships the evil one. Jesus replies, "Worship the Lord your God, and serve only him" (Matt 5:10). Jesus is not fooled by the temptations of wealth and power. He is centered, focused on doing the will and way of God. His example in the case of these forms of temptation is profound and speaks directly to those who follow a spiritual way in the contemporary world. We face the same temptations.

THE WILL OF GOD AS A WAY OF LIFE

As I reflect on these three temptations that were designed to steer Jesus away from his life calling, I sense that they contain, in story form, many of the ways I might rationalize my behavior and follow a way that would lead me away from the will of God. They invite me to make sure I know what it truly means to be led astray from the will of God. The phrase "will of God" does have the value of referring to the ways that are healthy, ones that will lead us in a positive direction and become foundational for the good life. It also suggests that there may be ways that will hurt us if we stray from the will of a loving God. Our task is to become sensitive to the guidance of God's will, consulting Scripture, of course, but also listening to sermons and teachers who have great wisdom. The phrase suggests that there is a positive way that will nurture and guide us as we walk, yet we still must make a discerning choice to follow what is truly the will of God. We have general guidance that comes from cultivating a more informed faith. As we find our way, we become hopeful, sensing that we have discerned the will of God. We are then able to translate our faith into a life of love. These three values—faith, hope, and love—are the true way, and the example of Jesus is the vivid expression and model of them in his life and ministry.

The letters of Paul illustrate so well the way these values become the foundation of the new movement we know as the faith of the early church. As the churches were founded, they needed constant attention in that the "church" was a new way of bringing people together around a common purpose and cause. Jesus certainly had the near equivalent of the church as people gathered around him, but he did move on to different places and did not stop for extended periods of time to be a long-term pastor or priest. In some ways, even Paul was inclined to be a traveling missionary more than a long-term pastor, although his focus was on establishing communities of faith. As we read his letters to these communities, we learn what he teaches about the life values that need to be present for a healthy church community.

A prime example of his pastoral guidance is found in the letters to the Corinthians. There were probably three letters that he wrote to this community of faith, although we now have only two, with the second letter containing what may be part of a third letter, the other part of the letter being lost. These letters provide us with a very good example of how the churches were formed and functioned. First Corinthians is an extended letter, and it deals with a range of issues that the Corinthians faced in the formation of this new community called the church. Paul did have a practical side, and in the early chapters of the letter, he deals with several problems that they faced. For example, he spoke to them about the divisions that occur in most any new organization and about the place of both wisdom and authority in the resolution of these concerns. He spoke about relationships and especially about marriage, its challenges and rewards. He addresses the place of the religious practices that were present prior to the conversion to Christianity, and whether believers should eat food offered to idols. He speaks about leadership and the role of leaders with spiritual gifts. He addresses whether it is possible to trust passages in the guiding literature that include prophecy, and he guides them about the practice of glossolalia, stressing the need for orderly worship. In short, he guides this new community of believers in a complex environment, a port city with all of its unique features and challenges.

Paul did help them with specific problems and issues, although he pauses toward the end of his first letter and speaks to them about a strong foundation: "But strive for the greater gifts. And I will show you a more excellent way" (12:31). He seems to be saying, "Yes, you will have a range of issues to deal with, but do not let the problems bog you down. There may be some challenges and confusion as you put this new community in place, but I want you to understand its foundation and its undergirding values. They are faith, hope, and love, and love is foundational."

SUSTAINING VALUES

Paul mentions faith first because it is foundational, and he then moves on to hope and love as the way to hike the pathway of faith. He lists these three sustaining values of a new church in part because they were just beginning their hike; they had just placed their faith in a new direction in life and did not have historical models and experienced leadership. In order to sustain their faith journey, they had to form a community of faith, a group of people with common beliefs and a shared commitment to ethical practices. As he wrote to them, Paul spoke of "faith" (*pistis, pisteuein),* by which he meant "to be true and trustworthy" in the verb form (Rom 3:21–31). For

Paul, true faith had three primary components: informed belief, trust in God, and corresponding action and way of life. This deep and profound value, with its three related commitments, was foundational.

Paul knew that there was a swirl of belief systems in the cosmopolitan city of Corinth, some linked to Greek and Roman philosophy, some from the underlying cultural norms of an established city in the Roman Empire, and some in the day-to-day life of each person who had a way of life that may have been either in conflict with or removed from the new faith orientation Paul was teaching. So, Paul writes to them, saying, "If I speak in the tongues of mortals and angels, . . . and if I have prophetic powers and understand all mysteries" (1 Cor 13:1–2), I may still be led astray. But true love came to us in the person of Jesus, and to place your faith in him will ground and sustain you. Love is the focus of this chapter in his letter, and the foundation of love is rooted in the deep belief that God is love. And the way you connect with the God of love is by *informed faith*. The heart of this new faith is the deep belief that God was in Jesus, who taught us how to live the life of love. Being informed and having an understanding of what God has done for us in Jesus is one vital dimension of faith.

The second dimension of this foundation, in addition to have an *informed* faith about God's presence in the life of Jesus, is a *commitment to follow the values inherent in the life and teaching of Jesus*. It is a bold step in that the life, teaching, and redemptive events of Jesus point us in a new direction and give us an alternative set of values from our culture; it will change our direction and the way we live. We are informed, and then we commit our lives to what we have learned. Paul is patient, knowing that his message on the surface may appear to be straightforward and easy to grasp. Yes, it is easy to affirm that we saw the love of God in the life and teaching of Jesus, but for us to follow in his footsteps requires an extraordinary commitment to make the Jesus event the ground of one's life. I identify with the Corinthians as I read Paul's letter to them. I admit that it took a while for me to understand that becoming a Christian meant a fundamental shift in my values and the flow of my life. I now understand that my faith gives me hope, and that my hope undergirds my quest to be a loving person.

I was somewhat innocent in my last year of high school as I was invited by friends to visit three different churches. I had very limited personal experience on which to draw as I sought to understand the new frame of reference for my life. The language in each one was slightly different, but gradually, wading through an evangelical voice, a mainline denominational voice, and a special youth group voice, I began to catch on. I am still learning with a doctorate in theology, sixty active years of Christian service, extensive research for faithful service and writing, and reflections on my extensive experience with Christians from all parts of the world. What I now try to do is to follow the trail of Jesus, to commit to a life and a way of understanding that he followed in all of its rich and sometimes threatening reality. I now have an informed faith, one still in a growth mode, but I sense that now I have years of experience and a thoughtful faith to guide me on the journey to follow the life and values inherent in the life of Jesus. This journey, tested, informed, and empowered, is filled with hope.

The third dimension of faith, of course, is that it is a way of life that has an action clause. It is more than just acceptance of a point of view, even more than thinking differently about life; it is to follow a comprehensive way of life. In my experience, it is a way of life rooted in faith, filled with hope, and now has an action clause. As the apostle Paul says, "If . . . , then . . . " (Phil 2:1–2). The third dimension of faith is to live a life filled with love, and a sense of God's presence encourages and empowers me to make love my highest priority. To live in obedience to the will of God is to be loving. Faith gave me hope, and now it empowers me to action. This notion of an active life based on following God's will and way now seems less daunting and more possible. I have the life of faith based on the embrace of the Jesus and years of study and experience, and I have made a commitment to make faith, hope, and love a way of life.

I want to pause briefly and underline the second word used by Paul to describe the life of faith: "hope" (*elpis, elpizein*). As I find my way in a confusing country and perilous world, I do not find it easy to flippantly say that I am hopeful. I live in a perilous world, the daily news is discouraging, and fear and worry threaten to eliminate the life of hope for millions of people. Yet the apostle Paul and those whom he taught, even in dire circumstances, were filled with hope. The foundation of their hope was the profound experience of God's loving kindness expressed in the stories of the Hebrew Bible and profoundly so in their understanding of Jesus. For them, as faithful to their Jewish faith, one story recorded in the Hebrew Bible and integral to their experience was very important: it was the freeing of the Hebrew people from slavery in Egypt. This story of liberation, coupled with the several stories of emancipation from other difficulties, gave them hope; they trusted that God was with them, would guide them, and would then lead them to a promised land and a way life based on justice and peace. This story and the several others in the Hebrew Bible made them hopeful. Their hope was based on:

1. The stories of liberation from slavery and bondage in the Hebrew Bible
2. The promise that God would continue to guide them to a bright future
3. The deep belief that Jesus the Christ had defeated evil in his life, his sacrificial death, and his resurrection
4. The promise that God will continue to guide and empower them as God did for Jesus
5. The reassurance that God's way will ultimately triumph

It is well and good to have faith in a loving God and a life filled with hope, yet the apostle Paul has one more word to share in describing the Christian way of life. It is the life of love. His comment about love is significant: "And now faith, hope, and love abide, these three; and the greatest of these is love" (1 Cor 13:13). As I introduce love into our discussion, I am keenly aware that the word ("love" in English, *agape* in Greek) has several meanings and even varies in meaning as it is translated into another language. In general, we think of love as expressed in the Greek "agape," meaning unconditional love, as an attraction to and caring for another regardless of what the other person (or persons) brings to the relationship. It has a comparable meaning to the English word "compassion," a genuine caring for the welfare of another. This emphasis does not necessarily erase the feeling of attraction, another understanding of our English word for love, but it does point clearly to a deep and profound concern for the life of another, or the lives of others. One cares for them even if they are not attractive and especially if they are in need of practical care.

THEOLOGICAL GUIDANCE

Let's consider the ways that we might show love, not just for our spouse or significant other, but for all those who come our way in life. How might we truly love other persons, our highest calling in life? Perhaps the best place to begin is to remind ourselves of the ground and foundation of love. Those of us whose faith is rooted in the biblical tradition affirm three theological affirmations about love:[3]

3. I realize that one religious family cannot claim to have the ownership of the human expression of love; in fact, many of the great religious traditions of the human family

1. The foundational theological affirmation is that God is love. Late in the first century, John of Patmos wrote the following to new Christians: "Beloved, let us love one another, because love is from God; everyone who loves is from God; everyone who loves is born of God and knows God. Whoever does not love does not know God, for God is love" (1 John 4:16). The apostle John is teaching that the very essence of God is love, and that as we participate in this love, we are related to and connect with God.
2. Also implied in the passage, and clearly stated in the early chapters of Genesis, is that we were created by love, in love, and to love. Jesus makes this observation on several occasions. When asked by a scribe, "Which commandment is the first of all?" Jesus answered, drawing upon his Hebrew Bible, "The first is, 'Hear, O Israel: you shall love the Lord your God with all of your heart, and with all of your soul, and with all of your mind, and with all of your strength.' The second is this, 'You shall love your neighbor as yourself.' There is no other commandment great than these" (Mark 12:28–31).
3. There is a third theological observation inherent in the teachings of the Hebrew Bible and Jesus: the affirmation that the primary meaning in human life is to join with God as a partner in the ongoing processes of creation and the transformation of society. We do so with self-giving love as our motivation; it is the expression of the loving God in our identity and way of life. Jesus sums it up as he quotes Leviticus in the Gospel of Mark: "The first is, 'Hear O Israel . . . you shall love the Lord your God with all of your heart, with all of your soul, with all of your mind, and with all of your strength.' The second is this, 'You shall love your neighbor as yourself.' There is no commandment greater than these" (12:29–31).

The apostle Paul affirms this central teaching of Jesus when he writes, "Let me show you a still more excellent way. If I speak in the tongues of mortals and of angels, but do not have love, I am nothing. If I give away all my possessions, and if I hand over my body so that I may boast, but do not have love, I gain nothing. Love is patient and kind; love is not envious or boastful or arrogant or rude. It does not insist on its own way. It is not

---

point to love as foundational for ethical life. It is present, of course, within Judaism (Jesus was a Jew), but present as well in nearly all of the religions of the human family, with Buddhism as a prime example.

irritable or resentful. It does not rejoice in wrongdoing, but rejoices in the truth. It bears all things, believes all things, hopes all things, and endures all things. . . . Faith, hope, and love abide, these three; and the greatest of these is love. Love never ends" (1 Cor 13:4–8).

This kind of love, as we have said, is unconditional, reaching across cultures, customs, classes, and castes, and even has the power to overcome behavior that offends and violates our most sacred values. It does so because we see the value of each person, even when their value is hidden behind behavior that may offend and violate our most sacred values. It does so because love focuses on the person behind the behavior, one created in the image of God and having infinite value. We do not condone the offense but reach out and give selflessly, even by the sacrifice of our own comfort. We extend the appropriate response that satisfies justice, meets the need of the other person, and heals the sickness of the soul and the body.

In this response, as our culture does too often, we should not focus exclusively on infatuation and attraction to the beautiful or even the profound but reach out in humility to help those in need. And, in particular, we care for our family, our spouse, or significant other, and we love them with the fullness of agape love. Fatigue, discomfort, difference of opinion, and stress may be present, but we still reach out in humility to love those near to us, giving the fullness of agape love.

THE IMPORTANCE OF LOVE IN GREEK PHILOSOPHY

It may be easy to say, as we read the New Testament, "Yeah, of course, Jesus says we ought to love. But he spoke to just a few followers." Might it have been just an isolated statement spoken to a sectarian group? The answer is no; in fact, his teaching on love is rooted in the Hebrew Bible, and then followed by people across cultures and centuries. Love has been lifted up as a central value for all humans across the ages and in a wide variety of sources. For example, Aristotle spoke about love in the context of describing friendships and illustrated his meaning by identifying three different kinds of friendship.[4] There is the lowest form of friendship, a false friendship in fact, in which we *use* those we know for our own personal gain. It is all right to

4. Aristotle spoke of love as expressed in friendship. His *Nicomachean Ethics* contains a clear account of his views on friendship. I am using the translation in *The Basic Works of Aristotle*, edited with an introduction by Richard McKeon (Aristotle, *Basic Works*, 927–1112).

expect a friend to assist us if we have a need, but when we view the friend as one whom we can manipulate for our own advantage, we violate the friendship. Another form of false friendship is when there is an exchange of mutual favors in normal everyday encounters, but a score is kept, and there is resentment or revenge if you are on the low side of the score. Aristotle would not affirm the phrase "I owe you one," as harmless as it may seem; a good friendship does not keep score, nor does it exploit the one who is viewed as a friend.

A second form of friendship mentioned by Aristotle, and another false form, would be to seek another's company solely for receiving enjoyment or pleasure. To enjoy one another is a gift, but we do not "use" or exploit people in order to receive this gift, but receive it in gratitude and appreciate what the other person brings to the relationship, understanding it as a gift that is given freely.

True friendship, which Aristotle affirms, is when there is mutual concern and active care. It may include being helped by and enjoying the presence of another person, and it is based on a deep and abiding trust that the other person cares about your welfare even as you care about the welfare of this person. It does not keep score.

This third form of relationship describes what we often mean in our culture when we say that we truly care for and are attracted to another person. At times, when we use the word as having the meaning of being attracted to another, it is often understood as physical attraction. Yet it is possible to use the word in a way that appreciates beauty and wisdom and not mean for the word to describe sexual attraction exclusively. Aristotle does use the Greek word "eros," which means attraction, enjoyment, and appreciation of another. It also meant in his time to have an attraction to an object such as a work of art, perhaps a great book, or part of nature we find especially beautiful.[5]

The word "eros" as it is used by Plato and Aristotle does not exclusively mean sexual attraction; it also may include an attraction to beauty in a person or in nature. It may be an attraction to that which is profound and insightful. Plato also used the word to describe the happy and fulfilled life: a life that is filled with the true, the good, and the beautiful. We can therefore speak about a good friendship as platonic in character. Erotic love is part of God's creation, and as we hike in the beauty of nature, we are filled with positive appreciation. We "come alive" when beauty is present, and this

5. See the classical book on this subject by Anders Nygren, *Agape and Eros*.

kind of attraction is the best form of friendship. It is good to appreciate the exceptional qualities and distinctive characteristics of the true friend, and to us the English word "love" is appropriate in reference to the friendship. It is good to take delight in their unique, insightful, and charming ways. It is especially good to love our spouse in this way as we share the delights and the responsibilities of life. We are drawn to them as there is the shared experience of goodness, truth, and beauty.

JESUS: TEACHING, FRIENDSHIP, AND HEALING,

Yes, it is true that Jesus placed a strong emphasis on agape, the love of those for whom we care, even if they are unattractive and do not invite a loving response because there are brilliant, beautiful, and caring. We walk, as Jesus did, with all kinds of people, in part because it is our calling as Christians to demonstrate unconditional love to all who come into our circle of nearness. Yet the emphasis is not exclusively sacrificial; it is more than just managing negative emotions when we encounter those who are unattractive. In fact, we discover, as we learn how to love without condition, that there is a measure of fulfillment in our loving. We learn that as we love in this way, we do the work of God and discover that love is integral to our fulfillment and well-being.

The Gospels have several stories where Jesus appears to be gratified that he has shown love to the sick, the unlovely, and the stranger. As we read the accounts of these stories in which Jesus expresses love, we discover that love takes several forms and is expressed in a particular way depending on the circumstances. I want to note five different kinds of encounters and responses in which the love of Jesus is expressed, although these five categories do not capture the fullness of his expressions of love; they are suggestive of the comprehensiveness and richness of his expressions of love. They are:

1. A response to the psychological and relational needs of the person
2. A response to the spiritual needs of the person
3. A response to the person caught in a situation of social injustice and unable to pursue a normal and constructive life
4. A response to the physical needs of the person
5. A wise response to the life-direction needs of the person

The Gospel of John records the story of Jesus meeting the woman of Samaria in the village of Sychar who is troubled in her relationships with men; in fact, she has been married five times and is currently living with a man who is not her husband (John 4:1–30). The setting in which Jesus encounters her is a common well, one with an interesting history and that was used as a common source of water for this Samaritan community. It was a non-Jewish community and had some similarities with "minority" people in one of our cities, people who suffered from discrimination because they were different. As Jesus paused there for a break, his disciples left him to rest while they went out to find food for a meal. Jesus encounters this Samaritan woman who had come to the well to get water. She was a minority person, not Jewish, and had a different background, perhaps even a slightly different language. This story illustrates the extraordinary capacity of Jesus to heal a psychologically damaged woman working on her sixth husband, a woman who suffered from her incapacity to form life-giving and lasting relationships. It is this ministry to troubled souls that he gives to his followers, one that heals the mistreated and broken-hearted person.

Jesus, accepting as he was, asks her for a drink of water. She is surprised and asks Jesus why an important person such as Jesus would ask her for drink. She was used to being ignored, perhaps even the victim of discrimination. Jesus, crossing cultures, shows no prejudice, and uses the gift of a drink of water to illustrate a universal spiritual truth, that God's love is for all people. He says to her, "Everyone who drinks of this water will become thirsty again, but those who drink the water I give them will never thirst again" (John 4:13–14). She responds and asks for this special kind of water. They speak together about her life, how she has had several husbands and life has been difficult. She longs for the universal water that will restore her life, and she finds it in her conversation with Jesus. She returns to her village as a transformed person and shares her new understanding, and her transformation improves relationships in her community, one outside of the Jewish context. Jesus tenderly loves her, easily breaks through social biases, demonstrates tender and understanding love to a troubled Samaritan woman, and restores her, and she is a new person who influences those in her little world.

Jesus continues to travel, and he meets a young man who appears not to be "needy" in that he has a good measure of wealth (Matt 19:16–26). He asks Jesus a variety of questions, each with the main point of how it is that we please God and obey the commandments. Jesus patiently and wisely responds when he asks about keeping the commandments, to which the young man replies that he has kept the commandments. Jesus then goes a bit deeper and asks the young man about his motivation to help those in need. Jesus may have sensed that this person was a bit self-righteous and perhaps needed to cultivate a deeper spiritual connection with God and to care for those in need. Jesus says, "If you wish to be perfect, go sell your possessions, and give the money to the poor, and you will have treasure in heaven; then come, follow me" (Matt 19:21). When the young man heard this word, he went away grieving, for he had many possessions. The ministry of Jesus invited all people, rich and poor, powerful and weak, educated and uneducated, to take seriously the invitation of Jesus to endorse the kingdom of God, the reign of God, and to follow him. This young man had a deep spiritual need, had become accustomed to wealth and possessions, and followed the commandments as an external act rather than an internal commitment to give himself to the will and way of God. Here, in this incident, we see Jesus addressing the deep spiritual needs of a person. As the young man walks away, Jesus reminds his disciples that it is "hard for a rich person to enter the kingdom of heaven" (Matt 19:23). that is, to give oneself to following the will and way of God. Jesus, in many of his encounters, addresses the spiritual needs of those whom he encounters.

Jesus also cared deeply about the physical well-being of those whom he encountered. Again and again, he would find a way to heal those who were sick and "paralyzed."[6] There is the time when Jesus heals a paralyzed person on the Sabbath, upsetting a few religious officials, and is questioned by authorities. He teaches about God's love, feeds many who listened to him teach, and continues to care for those who come his way. There is a Syrophoenician woman, a gentile, who senses that Jesus has removed "a demon" within her and made her well (Matt 17:18). Moving on, he cures a deaf man and a blind man. Many come to him for healing, help, and hearing about the transformational character of the presence of God in their lives. There is some conflict, as Jewish leaders wonder by what authority he has been approved to carry out his work of friendship, healing, and transformation. In time, as he returns to Jerusalem, those in authority can no long tolerate a person who is so free, so loving, so profound, and outside of the traditional ways of Judaism. Yet he continually speaks freely and with

6. Often in the New Testament, the word translated into English as "paralyzed" may have been broad enough to include other disabilities or illnesses.

new insight about unconditional love. It would not be long before the end. The trail of true love is a dangerous one.

A third form of ministry of Jesus was to heal the sick and to address the physical needs of those he encountered. He met many who were seriously ill, paralyzed and unable to move around, left on the edge of common life because of "leprosy," and suffered from physical distress. Matthew's Gospel (9:27–31) records the story of Jesus meeting two blind men who followed Jesus, and one cried out to him, "Have mercy on us, Son of David!" (Matt 9:27). Jesus entered the house where they were located, and asked them about their faith and whether they truly believed that Jesus could help them. They said, "Yes, Lord" (Matt 9:28). Then Jesus touched their eyes, and said, "'According to your faith let it be done to you.' And their eyes were opened" (Matt 9:29). He then asks them not speak about it because of the crowds who might arrive and block his access to continue his ministry. But they spread the good news, and Jesus had to cope with large crowds of people. Remarkably, he was able to address the crowds and teach them about love and care for those in need. His love often took the form of healing.

The Gospel of John also records the story of the woman who is caught in the combination of being poor, a woman, and in the context of social injustice, a fourth condition that was harmful to many of the people whom Jesus encountered (John 8:1–11). One day Jesus was teaching near the Temple, and the scribes and the Pharisees brought a woman to him who they claimed had been caught in the act of adultery. She may have been quite poor and, on occasion, received money from men seeking sexual pleasure. The scribes and Pharisees tested Jesus and asked him if they should stone her to death, a custom of distorted justice. Jesus, calm, sat near the woman, giving her comfort and protection. He then asked the men, "Let anyone among you who is without sin be the first to throw a stone at her" (John 8:7). And the men, sensing their own conflicted and hypocritical lives, left the setting one by one. Jesus, again with sensitive love, turned to the woman and asked where the men had gone. He asked the woman, "'Where are they? Has no one condemned you?' She said, 'No one, sir.' And Jesus said, 'Neither do I condemn you. Go your way, and from now on do not sin again'" (John 8:10–11). The ministry of Jesus was often expressed as sensitive love for those who were caught in poverty and social injustice. He sets this woman on a new course for her life. We do not have records about her future, but one might hope that with the help of Jesus, she may have found a constructive way to earn a living and perhaps found a way to be a part of caring community.

LESSONS FOR CONTEMPORARY CHRISTIANS

As we review the life and ministry of Jesus, and of course draw upon the endless number of sermons, articles, and books that have been written about his life and ministry, we are a bit overwhelmed with what he accomplished in such a short period of time in active ministry. It is not our purpose in this writing to presume to speak about all he accomplished. Yet a few observations, central to our theme of following Jesus, might be helpful and guide us. We may learn from his life about how we should live in our perilous times, how to help those who suffer, and how to invite people to receive the transforming gift of love.

I come before you, O Lord.
As the sun rises, may your hope rise up in me.
As the birds sing, may your love flow out of me.
As the light floods in this new day,
May your joy shine through me.
I come before you, O Lord,
And drink in this moment of peace.
That I may carry something of your hope, love, and joy
Today in my heart.
Amen

QUESTIONS FOR REFLECTION AND DISCUSSION

1. What was the purpose of the baptism of Jesus? Does it suggest that we too may gain insight and motivations about how we live our lives if we have a comparable experience?
2. What were the primary temptations of Jesus that may have prevented him from accomplishing his goals in life? Do you have comparable temptations that, if yielded to, might prevent you from achieving you goals in life?
3. How does one discern the God-given primary purpose and goals in one's life?

4. What are the undergirding values of your life that shape your behavior? How does love fit into your array of values?
5. What are the primary theological beliefs and foundational values that guide your life? How important is it to sense that these beliefs are really based on truth?

BOOKS TO CONSULT

1. Greg Baer, *Real Love: The Truth About Finding Unconditional Love and Fulfilling Relationships*
2. Denis de Rougemont, *Love in the Western World*
3. Anders Nygren, *Agape and Eros*
4. Stephen G. Post, *Unlimited Love: Altruism, Compassion, and Service*
5. Edward Collins Vacek, *Love, Human and Divine*

Chapter Five

Being Guided by the Mind and Heart of Jesus in Making Decisions in Our Daily Lives

One of the criminals who were hanged there kept deriding him and saying, "Are you not the Messiah? Save yourself and us!" But the other rebuked him, saying, "Do you not fear God, since you are under the same sentence of condemnation? And we indeed have been condemned justly, for we are getting what we deserve for our deeds, but this man has done nothing wrong." Then he said, "Jesus, remember me when you come into your kingdom." He replied, "Truly I tell you, today you will be with me in Paradise."

—Luke 23:39–43

WISDOM FROM JESUS ON THE CROSS

There are probably few times in our lives when we are more motivated to face and speak the truth than when we are at the point of death. At this time, we want to feel that we have lived well and, perhaps, to hear or sense the affirmation and gratitude from those near and dear to us. Feeling accepted and affirmed, we often move directly to an openness to the truth in the hope that we can clear up any old grudges and be free of guilt for our past mistakes. At the end of life, there may be a sincere sharing about past misdeeds, forgiveness, and then the sense that nothing stands between us and those dear to us: we are free to express a deep and true love. We want to be reassured that there is nothing that would prevent us from receiving love from those who are dear to us. We may even hope that those who have been inclined to judge us will forgive and affirm us. We are then at peace and have the hope to be received into the presence of God. We have integrity and are at peace.

I have been in settings in which I was chosen to be the minister performing the funeral service for one who has died. Most often, there is sadness, but also a deep appreciation of the one who has passed away. A few times I have officiated at a funeral service for one who has not been universally admired or even well-liked by those who were close to the person. As I spoke with these dear souls nearing death, I sensed that some did have burdensome guilt and wanted understanding and forgiveness at the end of life. They hoped to have time with those close to them, often family members, to ask for forgiveness for any offensive behavior, clear up any misunderstandings, and restore openness and full trust in these most important relationships.

They knew that trust was based on the presence of truth, respect, and empathy, and they wanted these values to be present. In these settings and conversations, the concern was often about forgiveness, overcoming any past misunderstandings, and gaining a clear conscience. When this had occurred, the dying one had less anxiety and a measure of peace about their condition. As others visited the one near death, there was often the sincere and deep expression of true love, made possible by careful discernment about what it was important to say and what could be left unsaid. The best of the visitors made the decision to bring *shalom* to these final moments, a peace that passes understanding, with little or no need for words, just unconditional love.

Sometimes, when one is near the end of life, there is still the temptation to be sure that there is no longer a lot of "unfinished business." Hopefully, it has been taken care of prior to these last hours. But if there is still some discomfort over the past, then empathy must be present; empathy leads to compassion, and compassion leads to forgiveness. The time to be open and honest about deep differences may have passed. It is very important that the visitor should not take over the agenda with self-references; one should be conscious that the one dying should be able to share from the heart. One hopes that whatever may have separated them from those they love has been wisely overcome by forgiveness and that the resulting respect is present. In these last moments, it is time to have the sense of being fully reconciled. Not infrequently, the dying person would share with me their hope that the service would be positive and have the dimension of the celebration of a life well lived, that all misdeeds have been forgiven and there has been reconciliation.

The lesson of this intense need for an open and loving context at the end of life is usually present in less intense ways in nearly all of life. Open and loving relationships are vitally important to us, and at times we need help in establishing and maintaining them. There are many sources of guidance on how to develop and maintain loving relationships; the book stores are full of them, and some guidance is immediately present in our newspapers and television programs. I read these sources with care and hope that I can learn how to be more loving. I am helped and often reminded that it is my faith in God and God's loving forgiveness and communication with the human family that are the best sources of guidance for me in establishing and maintaining open and loving relationships.

The prayerful words of the apostle Paul, "Let this same mind be in you that was in Christ Jesus," provide us with a working definition of what we mean as we seek to have love as the central value of our lives. It is true that this need for immediate divine guidance and empowerment may not surface in the critical moments of life or as one faces death. At these moments, we may need to be reminded of God's eternal love, and it is the pastor's responsibility to offer this gentle reminder and to reassure the one at the end of life that it has been present across the years of his or her life, although at times just below the surface.

I am persuaded that this awareness needs to be felt, affirmed, and visibly present across all of our waking hours, although especially so at the end of life. As possible, loving others should be a conscious choice we make in all of our relationships and should guide our behavior.[1] Nearly every day will present us with the challenge and opportunity to be loving; there will be the need for a compassionate atmosphere and important acts of love as each day unfolds.

I am motivated and guided by the teaching of the apostle Paul, who addresses this concern with the counsel to have the "mind" of Jesus. He says that to be like Jesus, to have his frame of reference, and to follow his example are the best ways to be empowered to love. The apostle Paul then expands his definition of what it means to have "the mind of Christ." I find his counsel very helpful, although difficult to follow in that it invites a major life change, a full transformation. It is more foundational than the somewhat limited advice that is often given: "Just do what Jesus did." This may be

1. Phil 2:1–11.

good advice at a given moment, but it does not clearly tell us about how to cultivate the deep attitude of compassion and spirit of love. The apostle Paul goes beyond the "be nice" advice and points to the deepest values of Jesus. He suggests that we can be changed by following his example and underlines how love was the essence or "mind" of Jesus, the deeply rooted center of who he was. Our goal is to cultivate the outlook and perspective of Jesus.

Paul offers his understanding of the mind of Christ by saying that as one goes through the day, as the situation changes, and as opportunities calling for our attention occur, the goal is not to be noticed and praised for our good work but to have compassion and sympathy deep within us. The word translated as "sympathy" means in part to "feel sorry" for those who suffer. But it goes well beyond just feeling sorry and points beyond just sympathy to profound empathy, the full identification with those who suffer. Paul illustrates what he means by this counsel:

a. Be humble and do not think of yourselves as "God" in a role of power and having all the answers. These self-centered attitudes inevitably lead to some form of exploitation and are driven by our ego needs. Rather, let unconditional love be always present and treat any troubled person who comes into your presence with compassion and humility (how can I help?), with sensitive and thoughtful care (tell me what is bothering you), and deep empathy (I understand, care, and will help).

b. Do nothing in these day-to-day settings that is motivated by selfish ambition or the need for attention, but focus on the needs and concerns of others. Give special attention to the person who, for a variety of reasons, has a deep need for a genuinely caring person to be with them. One does not want to be alone in moments of worry, fear, or deep crisis, although these feelings may cause us to retreat from relationships. In these moments, we want and need a person who listens to our feelings and concerns, one who understands, and one who is fully present with us.

c. It is all right and often necessary to care for the routine details of our lives in the presence of others. Life happens and it goes on! In the midst of the swirl, we may find it difficult to understand what is vitally important, and we often get bogged down in details. We do need to pay attention to details, but not at the cost of neglecting our needs and the needs of others. It is possible to manage the details of our work and even the mixture of feelings and needs that are present in our inner life and still be focused on caring for ourselves and loving others. In fact, as we look deep inside, we will discover that there is a great degree of empathy, although it may be hidden by our immediate needs. We in fact do have the capacity to care for those who are suffering as we carefully nurture the presence of God in our lives. Love then becomes the fruit of our God's Spirit within us, even as we care for the demands of our own life. It is possible to learn how to calmly care for your responsibilities and then identify with the person in front of you who needs love. It is possible to care for your needs without communicating that you don't have time to care for them and their needs. In fact, as we care for our needs, we are then freer to care for others. You can simply reassure them that you care, and that when you take care of important concerns, you will be back to help them. It will be possible to find time later to take care of their concerns. But, as far as possible, stay in the immediate present, listen carefully, and be attentive and genuinely empathic when you are with the person. There may be a deep need in the one with whom you are talking.

d. Those for whom we are caring do not need to hear our constant self-referencing,[2] following every comment they make with our problem that may be similar. It is not wise to tell them about all of our immediate concerns; they need our attention, empathy, and compassion.[3]

e. When there is a profound need in the person who is in our presence and with whom we are talking, we need to be ready to respond with understanding and the willingness to help. It was certainly the case again and again in the life of Jesus. As he spoke with people, he may have had his own deep needs, but he found time to care without undue distraction. His care was immediate. It is dramatically illustrated when Jesus responds to the person on the cross next to him who says, "Jesus, remember me when you come into your kingdom" (Luke 23:42). Jesus, enduring profound pain and suffering, still cares for the needy person by his side and responds to him, "Today you will be in Paradise" (Luke 23:43) It is not a statement about his own pain

2. Self-referencing is quite common, and we do need others to understand us and our concerns. But if it is a continual pattern of behavior, it robs the other person in the conversation of attention and true understanding. It is to say to them that your needs and interests are more important than their needs and interests.

3. Self-referencing may be the most common response that we make when someone comes to us with a problem.

and fears, but one guided by selfless love, a life attitude that hears and follows the apostle's words, "Let each of you look not to your own interests, but to the interests of others" (Phil 2:4).

WISDOM FROM JESUS ON SOCIAL CLASS

It may be easy in times of stress and worry to focus almost exclusively on one's own problems. We all have plenty of them and, at times, are inclined to speak about them. It is often difficult for us, given our needs, to turn to the needy person in our circle and, with empathy, hear them and help them with care and wisdom. It is even more difficult to focus on the needs of those who are not like us, have a different language and come from a different culture, and who are outside of our circle of comfort. To speak with and care for strangers, those in a different social class, those from a different culture, country, and language, and those whose bodies are ill or broken, may be difficult for us. The counsel of Paul, certainly aware of the profound differences among human beings, is clear that we should help all troubled people as we are able. His counsel goes beyond our conversation with the random individual who is much like us and whom we meet at a given moment on a busy day. A friendly greeting, a "hello," may be all that is necessary. He is saying that to have "the same mind . . . in you that was in Christ Jesus" means that as we are able, we need to care about all people, and especially those who live in difficult and unjust settings. Both the model and the teaching of Jesus challenge us to be ready to go outside of our comfort zone to engage in caring actions of love.

Wherever he went, he was especially sensitive to those who suffered. He saw clearly the poverty, the lack of food, the sick people, the personal crises, and the unjust social conditions in his public ministry. He was at ease with those from a different culture and setting; he honored the good Samaritan in his parable and helped the woman at the well. In fact, he was a victim of injustice in the last days of his life, and yet he cared for the soldiers who put him on the cross, saying, "Father, forgive them; for they do not know what they are doing" (Luke 23:34). To have the same outlook as Jesus, to sense who Jesus was and then to have his mind and heart, is to be ready to challenge those social structures that are unfair and help the person who is suffering from injustice. He truly loved, and we are invited to follow his example.

Paul is also implying that it may be our time to take responsibility to attempt to change those practices in our settings that discriminate against those who are different—who live in poverty, have little education, are born with a handicap, perhaps blind and disfigured, have limited access to education, or are without sufficient income to take care of basic needs. He lived his life in the middle of human struggle and need and had time for those who came to him for help.

He thoughtfully cares for those who were ignored and was viewed by those in power or the representatives of a foreign government as a nuisance. He cared for those in deep need who, because of class structures, lack of income, and different languages and cultures, were mistreated and ignored. Luke records the comments of Jesus that call attention to the unjust class structures and the prejudices regarding those who were different that existed in his time. For example, he illustrates his awareness and understanding of prejudice as he tells his disciples the story about those invited to a wedding banquet and where they might sit for the ceremony.

> When he noticed how the guests chose the places of honor, he told them a parable. "When you are invited by someone to a wedding banquet, do not sit down at the place of honor, in case someone more distinguished than you has been invited by your host; and the host who invited both of you may come and say to you, 'Give this person your place,' and then in disgrace you would start to take the lowest place. But when you are invited, go and sit down at the lowest place so that when your host comes, he may say to you, 'Friend, move up higher'; then you will be honored in the presence of all who sit at the table with you. For all who exalt themselves will be humbled, and all those who humble themselves will be exalted." (Luke 14:7–14)

Friends and family at the wedding feast, of course, may get to sit at the front, but do not neglect those on the lower end of the income level and social class. They, too, may be friends of the couple who are getting married. Honor them as well and seat them where there is space, without discrimination. There was clear discrimination in these kinds of events in the time of Jesus, and he uses the story of a wedding feast to make his point. He talks about those sitting in the place of honor, whether it is appropriate for them to sit in that section, and suggests that it would be wise not to assume you are more important than others. It would be better to wait to see if you will be invited to sit in that section, not to go there to show others how important you are. He then counsels his listeners not to invite just relatives and neighbors, knowing others may want to be included as well. Instead, "when you give a banquet, invite the poor, the crippled, the lame, and the blind. And you will be blessed, because they cannot repay you, for you will be repaid at the resurrection of the righteous" (Luke 14:12). He underlines the spirit of humility and the need to care for those who are left out in the social structures. Jesus is inviting everyone to come to the "banquet of life"; this means that all people should be treated fairly by the laws, have the opportunity for a good education, have access to a healthy diet, be able to receive good medical care, and have the opportunity to be treated fairly by the "system." All humans have value and, as far as possible, should be treated with care and justice.

WISDOM FROM JESUS FROM THE SERMON ON THE MOUNT

The writers of the Gospels give us an account of the guidance Jesus gave to his contemporaries about how to live wisely and well. These words of wisdom are present in all four Gospels, each with a slightly different starting point and purpose depending upon the setting and the needs of those who listened to him teach and saw his behavior. For us to have a better understanding of his "mind" or outlook as he went through each day, it is helpful for us to know the context of the accounts that are provided for us in the Gospels. We gain a better understanding if we know the language, culture, particular setting, and circumstances in which he taught. Fortunately, we do have reasonably good records about the time and place where he lived and taught. To know the history of the people and the languages they spoke is enlightening.

Yet it is the New Testament, and the Gospels in particular, that inform us about his unique way with people and the specific content of his teaching. The context is the first century in Israel-Palestine, a setting with a particular culture, shaped by the Jewish way of life and the indigenous Palestinian ethos and language. There is a mixed indigenous population, Palestinian and Jewish, and the presence and control of a foreign government, the Roman Empire. The information about these different groups and cultures gives us a frame of reference and historical context within which we seek to understand and interpret the accounts of the actions and teaching of Jesus.

In addition, we do have relatively good information about the life and teaching of Jesus and how these records, the Gospels, come to us. There has been a careful and extensive process that gives us good information about the setting in which Jesus lived and undertook his mission.[4] The earliest of the Gospels, the Gospel of Mark, was written in the later part of the 60s, and it tends to trace the teaching and public events of the life of Jesus in a straightforward way. There is interpretation, of course, because the account has the purpose of informing and nurturing the faith of later generations. Mark, without an extensive development of the meaning of the events and teaching of Jesus, provides us with a reasonably good record of the public life of Jesus.[5] Mark's account was used and consulted by the writer of the Gospel of Matthew, and Matthew, to whom we attribute authorship of the Gospel with his name attached, provides us with additional material, including the Sermon on the Mount, perhaps our best organized record of the teaching of Jesus. Luke also had some of the material in Mark's Gospel in front of him as he wrote his Gospel. But he, too, had additional records of the teaching of Jesus, and, as a non-Jewish author, has a slightly different perspective on the Jesus event.

There was also an oral tradition, a very important information source in a nonliterate culture. There was a well-preserved oral account that contained important information about the life and teaching of Jesus. It was persevered by teaching and preaching in the small churches that had been formed. Much of this material would have been available to Mark and Matthew. Luke had access to some of this information, as well, and also uses the material of the accounts in Mark and Matthew, as he writes his Gospel. Luke does shift the focus slightly as he writes his account of the meaning of the events in the life of Jesus from a non-Jewish perspective. The Gospel of John, somewhat different from the three synoptic Gospels, provides some factual information on the life of Jesus, but is much more concerned with meaning. John's Gospel provides us with the beginning of a theological frame of reference for understanding Jesus.

It is helpful for those who now read and interpret these accounts to know how the material used by authors of the Gospels influenced their accounts, how authentic these accounts were, and how we may use the Gospels to provide an accurate account of the life, teaching, and meaning

4. Of course, as with all historical writing, those who write the history weren't present in the setting about which they write. Therefore, with great care, we gain our understanding from our historical records about his life and the content of his teaching. Neither CNN nor Fox were there.

5. It is not a complete record in that there is no account of the birth and early life of Jesus.

of Jesus. These resources have been and are being used by those who write the story of Jesus.[6]

What we have are different accounts of much of the same teaching and events, although the author of the Gospel of John, written later than the other Gospels, has a slightly different approach and goal as he writes. Yet all four Gospels do have much in common. The representatives of the Christian church and many others come, then, to these sources of information and other historical material with the need for a careful reading and a sound process of interpretation.[7]

As we read the Gospels in order to understand the life and teaching of Jesus, it is wise, as we have implied, to read them with an awareness that they were written by different authors at different times and with each Gospel having a slightly different purpose. The authors of the Gospels used some written material and had access to the sayings and stories that were in an oral tradition.[8] So, we turn to the records we have and, with care, bring the knowledge we have of the life and teaching of Jesus to our present setting in order to guide us in our beliefs and practices.

THE SERMON ON THE MOUNT: GUIDANCE FOR LIVING WISELY AND WELL

We turn first to what we now call the Sermon on the Mount, a wonderful collection of many of the teachings of Jesus. It is a composite of material, given by Jesus in oral form at different times and places and only later collected and put in written form. It is a remarkable collection, full of great wisdom and insightful guidance.

6. There has been an extensive study since the middle of the nineteenth century to determine the reliability of the accounts we have of Jesus and his teaching. They are filled with descriptions of events and a variety of thoughtful conclusions. Scholars of the New Testament range in their views, with some having full trust in the accounts and others suggesting that we do not have sufficient information to fully trust all the theological conclusions of the traditional teaching of the Christian church.

7. There are those who essentially trust this material as accurate and others that remind us that the material is subject to the best practices of critical history. Words such as "inspiration" are often used by the more conservative side of the church, and others place more confidence in using the best tools of critical historical study in order to discern how the material may be traced back to the life of Jesus and how it should be understood.

8. Luke notes that he had some written material available to use as he wrote his Gospel (1:1–4).

Authorship is attributed to Matthew, a disciple of Jesus, and it is likely that there were others who helped as material was collected. The Sermon on the Mount reflects an editor with a command of Greek and rabbinic training in how to preserve and study these important documents. We are grateful to Matthew and other wise and informed people who were instrumental in preserving the teaching of Jesus in this careful way.

This collection of this material, which Jesus taught in an oral form, likely was spoken at different times in a setting close to what may have been Peter's home on the Lake of Galilee. There is a monastery that is present on these hills above the water, and those who make their home in the monastery have an extraordinary setting in which to study, reflect, pray, and serve.

As one visits, it is easy to imagine that Jesus could have been heard by relatively large crowds. The setting would have given him a place near the top of a hill to speak, with his listeners sitting below him or across from him. What we call the Sermon on the Mount is a collection of material that Jesus likely taught in these hills near the northwest corner of the Sea of Galilee and the village called Capernaum.

It was not one sermon, but a collection of material he taught over an extended period of time. The remembered material was put together in written form much later, and we now have it in a succinct collection that teaches the sacred values of life and the ethical norms of the responsible disciple. This teaching, perhaps more than any other collection, gives us a profound and deeply inspiring account of what Jesus taught about what we now call the spiritual life of the Christian. This material is a wonderful resource for how we should live our lives as Christians, yes, but also for all who seek to live the good and true life in a spiritual way. It may be one of our best records of the mind and heart of Jesus, and it represents the way we seek to understand and respond to the apostle Paul's urging that we seek to live as those having the heart of and mind of Jesus.

What is called the Sermon on the Mount is found in the Gospel of Matthew, chapters 5–7. It is not one sermon, but a collection of the teachings of Jesus, put in its present form over an extended period of time. It is judged as being a relatively true account of the teaching of Jesus, carefully preserved in oral form and later put into writing. It was not unusual for important teaching to be preserved in oral form, given that there were no printing presses. In time, the material was written, although much later after it was presented in oral form.[9] The teaching of Jesus was judged to be

9. The oral form of preserving important information was reasonably thorough and

exceedingly valuable in providing extraordinary wisdom about life. After he spoke, his listeners would often repeat his teaching and share it with others. We are most fortunate to have this collection of his teaching, thought to have been put in writing by Matthew.[10]

Blessedness: Matthew 5:1–12

Matthew begins his account of the teaching of Jesus with the comment that as one opens their heart to God, they enter into a state of blessedness (a state of deep peace, happiness, and honor), regardless of their setting and condition in life. Undergirding these statements of blessedness is the metaphor of the kingdom of God, the idea that one who has faith in God and invites God's presence into their lives is content and at peace as a citizen in God's realm (5:3–12). The analogy of a kingdom may not have been our choice, but it was a way for readers to understand that the one in power has invited people into a kingdom that has values and ways of living that enable and empower them to flourish. It is available even to the poor, the disenfranchised, and those who suffer.

1. "Blessed are the poor in spirit, for theirs is the kingdom of heaven" (5:3). They have citizenship and live with love and justice of God's kingdom or realm. Even the poor may be at peace as those who belong to the one who has power and is in control of all of life.
2. Those who mourn also have this great privilege and deep happiness, for they shall find comfort for their loss by the presence of God (5:4).
3. The meek, those who are always left out and set aside, shall be like those who have everything; they shall "inherit the earth." All the beauty and goodness of the earth shall be theirs (5:5).
4. And those who long for righteousness shall find it in the realm of God. True goodness, pure love, and life-giving truth shall be theirs (5:6).
5. "Blessed are the merciful"; they, too, will receive mercy (5:7).

accurate, a way for a nonliterate culture to preserve its history and wisdom of the past in order to guide them in the present.

10. Matthew is given credit for the collection, but its current form may be the product of the normal process of review and editing by those with knowledge of Greek and familiarity with the form of the rabbinic literature.

6. Those who are pure in heart, of course, will even be able to "see" God, be in God's presence and know it intimately. To be pure is to see clearly, without that clutter that clouds the perspective of those without a pure heart (5:8).
7. Peacemakers, those who make life better for thousands of people, will be the children of God in this kingdom. They will live at peace with all others (5:9).
8. Those who have difficulty and are persecuted will be honored as children of God (5:10).
9. So, rejoice, you are blessed by God even in the midst of the difficulties of life. Life can be managed, and there is great joy and peace, deep satisfaction, and comfort for those who belong to God (5:11, 12).

Those in the kingdom of God will know who they are and how they shall live. They shall be filled with the peace of God that passes all understanding (Phil 4:7).

Identity: Matthew 5:13–20

1. You are like salt that enriches taste, giving gratification to all those around you (5:13).
2. You are like light that enables people to see, empowering them to live wisely and well (5:14).
3. You are like a prophet who is righteous and who teaches others about the dangers of life in an unjust society (5:17–20).

Your behavior as a citizen of God's kingdom will be wonderful and a model for all to follow.

Behavior: Matthew 5:21–48

1. Your life won't be driven by anger. Anger has little value, and it is best to be reconciled to your brother and sister and live in harmony with them (5:21–26).

2. Adultery: It is very important to be faithful to one's spouse; faithfulness creates trust, which is the essence of love and the heart of a good and rich relationship (5:27–30).
3. Divorce: As far as possible, stay true to your promises to your spouse, even when it gets difficult (5:31–32).
4. Oaths: Be true to your promises; good relationships are built on trust. A lot of words are not necessary and may have little meaning or ability to provide the foundation of a good relationship (5:33–37).
5. Concerning retaliation: Turn the other cheek and go the extra mile; forgive and build a relationship of understanding and care (5:38–42).
6. Enemies: Though it may be difficult, love your enemies and pray for those who persecute you. It is the way to build a better world (5:43–47).

Spiritual Practices: Matthew 6:1–34

1. Give alms without calling attention to what you give. Give with a pure heart and with no need for your gift to be recognized by others.
2. Pray as the Lord's Prayer teaches you, sincerely and often. The Lord's prayer is the model. It contains all the essential elements of maintaining a deep and pure relationship with God.
3. Fast as a means of cultivating discipline, but do it privately. It is important to have discipline in one's life, and fasting is a way to prepare oneself to have the discipline and courage to follow a principle and be true to one's commitment.
4. Use your money wisely. Do not waste it; rather, use it for the good of others.
5. Follow the light. It reveals God's presence and a direction that enables us to see clearly and do what is best for all.
6. Do not worry. God is with us, our faith in God will sustain us, even in the midst of troubles and worries.

Relationships and Practices: Matthew 7:1–29

1. Do not judge unfairly. Treat others with respect, just as you would like to be treated.
2. Respect what is holy.
3. Ask God for help, and do it sincerely.
4. Do unto others as you would have them do unto you (the Golden Rule).
5. Have integrity: enter the narrow gate, choose the good fruit.
6. Be sincere and without hypocrisy.

It would be hard to overstate the value of these teachings; they have undergirded the life of millions of people across the centuries. They represent the mind of Jesus, which we seek to have as the foundation of our live.

QUESTIONS FOR REFLECTION AND DISCUSSION

1. What is meant by Jesus when he uses the expression "the kingdom of God"?
2. How does one become a citizen of the kingdom of God?
3. What are the blessings or beatitudes of being invited to be a citizen of the kingdom of God?
4. What are the values and responsibilities of being a citizen of the kingdom of God?
5. Of all of the teachings of Jesus contained in the Sermon on the Mount, which one is your favorite? The most challenging? The ones that you have incorporated into your life? The ones which are the most difficult to practice?

BOOKS TO CONSULT

1. G. R. Beasley-Meyer, *Jesus and the Kingdom of God*
2. Günther Bornkamm, *Jesus of Nazareth*

3. Elias Chacour, *The Sermon on the Mount: An Invitation to Receive and Advance the Reign of God*
4. Gerhard Lohfink, *Jesus of Nazareth: What He Wanted, Who He Was*
5. Ben F. Meyer, *The Aims of Jesus*

Chapter Six

Applying the Mind and Heart of Jesus to the Context of One's Life in Our Perilous Contemporary World

At that time the disciples came to Jesus and asked, "Who is the greatest in the kingdom of heaven?" He called a child, whom he put among them, and said, "Truly I tell you, unless you change and become like children, you will never enter the kingdom of heaven. Whoever becomes humble like this child is the greatest in the kingdom of heaven. Whoever welcomes one such child in my name welcomes me."

—Matthew 18:1–5

Jesus was fond of providing basic guidance for those whom he met along the way in life. Life was not easy for those whom he met. As he traveled in the region of Israel-Palestine, he was increasingly surrounded by people who longed to hear him and learn from him. They wanted help with their lives! He did help them by providing profound insight and wisdom for the routine of life, and as noted in the passage above, every moment can be simple joy as we encounter others with a humble spirit and the congruent innocence of a child.

All too frequently, life is a challenge for us. For example, we enter into a conversation with a friend often with mixed feelings. Perhaps we judge them and then our agenda is to change the other person, win an argument, and get our way. The counsel of Jesus for this sort of daily contact with others is to be like a child, one without a hidden agenda, but with authenticity and a simple and immediate presence. It is to be humble and real in the moment and, as far as possible, to love those who come our way.

In several sections of the New Testament, as we read about the way Jesus interacted with others, we note that he had integrity and listened carefully. He had the directness of a child, spoke the truth, and responded with grace and understanding in his day-to-day encounters. He was real, even as an innocent child is real. He was in touch and in tune, and invites his followers, as they go through life, to have this humble and authentic presence. He went on to say that such a person is better able to encounter and experience God in their lives.

Jesus used the notion of the kingdom to speak about the presence of God, using the language of the kingdom of heaven or the realm of God.[1] It is in this realm where the fullness of God is present, and it is possible to be with God with a simple and pure act of faith. Such a person, living in this realm, begins the journey of life in a pure and authentic way, true to oneself, living with integrity and the capacity to manage the domains and challenges of life as an authentic person. When we are in the presence of such a person, there is the sense of being with one whom we can trust. As they meet us, and sense that we, too, are authentic, then a true and loving relationship will occur. In fact, Jesus goes on to say, "Whoever welcomes one such child in my name welcomes me" (Matt 18:5). Jesus is teaching us that this way of life, being a true person, one with integrity, one who is authentic, and one who has the spirit of love and compassion, is one of grace and peace.

I have to admit that to live with this kind of integrity has not been all that easy for me. It was a way of being that was not modeled for me in my childhood. I want to say, however, that I am grateful to my parents and others close to me that I was never rejected and always felt that I was part of the family. So, I am grateful for the way my family gave me this sense of belonging as part of my identity. Yet I have also had to overcome some of the values and ways of managing life that were modeled for me and that have been problematic.[2]

1. The metaphor of kingdom may not have been our choice as a concept to make a point, but it would have been understood by the contemporaries of Jesus that God is loving and powerful and invites humans to be citizens of the kingdom or the realm of God. God is able to give us a rich and true life as citizens.

2. I do not want to blame my family for my challenges; they are part of life regardless of family influence. Our upbringing, however, does shape the way we seek to be mature in a perilous world.

As I have reflected on my experience and read with great interest the stories about Jesus and his teaching, I have learned that Jesus, in his relationships and the flow of his life, was guided by deep and profound convictions and values, and he was consistent in honoring them and being true to them in every aspect of his life. Many others across the centuries, scholars and deeply spiritual teachers of wisdom, have had undergirding values as well. I have learned a great deal from these saints and scholars, although Jesus has been my primary model. I would like to summarize my learning about the values of Jesus in four words or concepts that became the foundational values that guided him in his actions and teachings.[3] I also want to stress that these four values, understood in a broad way, can serve as the foundation for personal and corporate statements of ethics.

TRUTH

Jesus cared deeply about truth in all of its different manifestations. He seldom spoke about it in the form of a simple definition but illustrated it in all that he believed, said, and did. He was not a philosopher in the sense of Plato or Kant, who spoke about truth in the abstract; rather he was one who illustrated the truth by what he said, by what he did, and as he spoke with his contemporaries. It was the truth of a profound teacher who shares insights with listeners and learners. It was the truth of a great prophet who spoke boldly about injustice. It was the truth of a humble healer who came alongside of those who suffered from a variety of physical and psychological illnesses. He gave them understanding about their suffering from poverty and hunger and healed their broken bodies. He lived and spoke liberating truth. He was authentic and truthful in all he said and did. He was authentic in all aspects of life.

In particular, Jesus endorsed the best expression of spiritual truth that was foundational for his contemporaries in Israel-Palestine. He shared his Hebrew faith with them and spoke to them about liberation and salvation. He deeply believed that the one true God would guide and help them. Jesus spoke in the language they understood and illustrated his message from the book (the Hebrew Bible) that they shared. He had integrity in all he said and did.

3. I have seen lists having over ten values, while others have said that the one value, such as love, was foundational. The lists vary and often reflect the life setting of the interpreter. My list reflects my convictions as I have studied the life and teachings of Jesus.

Yet he was more than just a messianic figure for the Jewish community; he also spoke the truth to Romans who ruled the region and to a variety of communities that had their own language, customs, and history. There was in this teacher, prophet, and healer a universal truth that crossed all the cultural, historical, and language barriers of his contemporaries. His life and teaching were revolutionary.[4]

Prior to the rise of critical historical study, Jesus was largely understood in the categories and descriptions of him in the Gospels, although from the start, there were those who doubted the literal truth of the biblical record. There were those who questioned the more literal description of the so-called miracles of Jesus. Accepting the literal truth of the Gospels became even more difficult to sustain when Jesus began to be studied with the tools of the critical historical method. This shift toward careful historical study remains, with some interpreters suggesting that we can know very little about Jesus from the Gospels. Yet there continue to be many others who say that the access to Jesus is quite difficult, but with careful study, there is still a great deal that we can know about him. The debate continues among scholars of the New Testament, and there is now some agreement about what we can know from historical study.[5]

The Christian church, for the most part, continues to affirm that what we have in the Gospels gives us an adequate foundation for belief. Those who proclaim the message are sincere in their ministry, believing the record, with careful study, contains the truth. However, many of those starting within the context of faith have joined in the debate on how much we can know from historical study. This historical study of Jesus has been named the "quest of the historical Jesus," the title of the book by Albert Schweitzer, published in 1910 in English.[6]

As one might expect, there was a new movement in Jesus studies that occurred in response to the partial consensus in New Testament scholarship

4. See, for example, the scholarly and thoughtful book by John Dominic Crossan, *Jesus, A Revolutionary Biography.* See as well the biography of Jesus by Bart D. Ehrman, *Jesus: Apocalyptic Prophet of the New Millennium*, and the book *The Prophet Jesus and the Renewal of Israel: Moving Beyond a Diversionary Debate* by Richard Horsley.

5. My observations here cover broad trends and are based on a lifetime of study. I am indebted to many fine New Testament scholars who have taught me. I am especially grateful to Marcus Borg, John P. Meier, and N. T. Wright. Their scholarship and deep faith have taught and guided me as I have studied the life and teachings of Jesus, as have the other authors who works I have cited.

6. Schweitzer, *Quest of the Historical.*

that it was very difficult to get back behind the Gospels and discover the historical Jesus. This new movement reached its full bloom in the first half of the twentieth century, and it maintained that there was sufficient historical material that would continue to make Jesus and his teaching relevant to the circumstances of nearly any period in history or distinctive culture. It is an expression of historical truth, and it is available to us with a careful and scholarly reading of the Gospels. However, the claim of his divinity cannot be proved by historical study. This belief should be left in the purview of the church and to those with faith, suggesting that faith gives one an access to spiritual truth. The belief in his divinity, however, cannot be determined by scholarly research.

What can be discerned in this vast array of careful and scholarly research is that the human Jesus was much like he is described in the Gospels, although the debates about his healing miracles, etc., continue to be discussed. What does come through to us is his integrity and deep devotion to help those in need. We have what we need when we say that he was truthful, had integrity, and was compassionate and authentic in all of his dealings; he was truthful and loving in all aspects of his life.

LOVE

Jesus, as far as we know, was truthful in all aspects of his life. He had integrity, spoke the truth, and lived authentically in reference to what he understood as the nature, presence, and teaching of God. He followed with great integrity the belief in God, understood by him in the categories of first-century Judaism. At the heart of this view is that God is love and wants those who put their faith in God to give love the highest priority in their lives. Matthew records a conversation he had with a lawyer (a Pharisee): "'Teacher, what commandment in the law is the greatest?' He said to him, 'You shall love the Lord your God with all of your heart, and with all your soul, and with all your mind. And the second is like it: 'You shall love your neighbor as yourself. On these two commandments hang all the law and the prophets'" (Matt 22:36–40).

As one might expect, there are questions about whether Matthew's Gospel records a true conversation. There is little to suggest that it was just a random view that the author of Matthew's Gospel throws in to make the account readable and interesting. Yes, there is important research that needs to be done in order to assess the accuracy of this statement, but when all the study is completed, there is a strong consensus that Jesus likely spoke these words about the priority of love. They represent who he was and what he believed.

The larger question of whether they are authentic has to do with what is meant by the words he may have spoken. He did not speak them in Greek, more likely in Hebrew, although Aramaic was also spoken. As they are translated from the Hebrew into Greek, the chosen word, familiar to us, is "agape" (*agapan*), which has the meaning of loving without condition, being self-giving, and remaining steadfast and loyal in one's relationships and way of life.

As we read the stories about Jesus in the Gospels, we see that he was accepting to all who came his way, even when they were not attractive or easy to be with.[7] Time and again, Jesus meets those who are ill, abused, angry, and nearly helpless. There were those who challenged Jesus (Pharisees who were lawyers in power), but even in these encounters, he accepts them as people of worth, although on occasion he calls into question some aspects of their behavior. Yet he honors them, receives them, speaks with them, and treats them with respect. His love is not conditional. The same is true as he meets those who are ill, lonely, and lost. He helps them and heals them. There are several descriptions of Jesus meeting people who were not easy to love.

Mark, in his Gospel, describes a person with a serious mental illness who is called "the Gerasene demoniac" (Mark 5:1–21). The story is in Matthew and Luke as well. Gerasene, a region located on the eastern side of the Lake of Galilee, was visited by Jesus in his active ministry. On one visit, he was met by a person who was severely troubled, one who had been living in a graveyard among tombs; it was a form of imprisonment. He had been chained there but had broken out of his shackles when he learned that Jesus would be in the region. When Jesus came near, this person ran toward Jesus and began to shout, "What do you have to do with me, Jesus, Son of the Most High God?" (Mark 5:7). Perhaps he thought that the presence of Jesus might make a difference in his life. Jesus greeted him and asked his name, and he replied that he was called Legion, suggesting that he was filled with evil spirits (a legion of them). Jesus did not turn away, but in his unique power, sent what they considered to be the evil spirits into a heard of swine, and in the process, the swine rushed down the hill into the sea and

7. He did express some anger and strong disagreement with the Pharisees and Sadducees.

drowned. Before Jesus left to return to his location on the other side of the lake (sea), the man spoke with him and asked if he could follow Jesus. Jesus said that he should stay in his home area and tell the story of his healing, and "how much Jesus had done for him." It is next to impossible to interpret all aspects of this story with contemporary insights on his mental illness. But it is possible to say that Jesus healed a very sick man who was alienated from the people in his region because of his serious mental illness. What is remarkable is that others had given up in the attempt to heal him. Jesus, however, accepted him into his presence and cared for him in a special way, and the man was in some way healed by this encounter. It is remarkable that being fully accepted and acknowledged by Jesus had a such a profound effect.[8] The sick man had heard about Jesus and his healing power, and when he encountered Jesus, he was transformed. There have been various interpretations of this unusual event; most suggest that the sense of being treated with unconditional love by a famous person was a profoundly healing experience. Love does make a difference in human relationships.

It was not Jesus's practice to just leave those whom he met alone, with the assumption that they would find their way. As a way of overcoming the loss of the presence of the one who loves, it was and is important to suggest the true love continues, even if schedules take us in different directions. There is an active response that is self-giving, one in which he expresses a deep concern and genuine caring that will continue, even if schedules take us in different directions. Yet it is possible to continue to feel loved, if the one who loves us in the present expresses the love with great sincerity, self-giving, and the promise that the love will continue. Jesus loves in a way that reassures those he loves that he will stay engaged in loving even though absence is inevitable. This kind of love is present in a good marriage!

One might also interpret his interactions with the power brokers within the Jewish hierarchy as expressions of the backside of love—a challenge to negative behavior or the misinterpretation of a religious practice, and even a gentle reminder that their behavior may not represent their deep religious commitments and values. In his own unique ways, as we read the accounts in the Gospels, the love of Jesus is active, takes time and patience, and can be exhausting. But Jesus, as we read the Gospels and interpret them with care, appears to have been one who loves, not just with words and a passive retreat, but with a self-giving action that costs him time, energy, and the

8. Biblical scholars and preachers have had difficulty explaining what happened that day, but we can rejoice that loving acceptance had such an impact on a very ill person.

cost of letting his own needs and concerns remain in the background. He is an active lover, and his love will continue. Matthew writes that "Jesus went throughout Galilee, teaching in their synagogues and proclaiming the good news of the kingdom and curing every disease and every sickness among the people. So, his fame spread throughout all Syria, and they brought him all the sick, those who were afflicted with various diseases and pains . . . and he cured them. And great crowds followed him from Galilee, the Decapolis, Jerusalem, Judea, and from beyond the Jordan" (4:23–25).

His love appears to be endless. Jesus doesn't retreat or run for cover when to love a vast number of people is difficult and demands a continuing presence, even though to remain engaged in the relationship creates discomfort, worry, or even a push back from the one who is being loved. Jesus had a special relationship with his disciple whom we know as Peter. There are several small stories about how Jesus, patient as he was, loved Peter when he was not all that lovable. One dramatic illustration of the love of Jesus, steadfast to the end for Peter, is when Peter is present at the arrest of Jesus but does not want to be identified with him for fear of being arrested. "Then they seized him and led him away into the high priest's house. But Peter was following at a distance. When they had kindled a fire in the middle of the courtyard and sat down together, Peter sat among them. Then a servant-girl, seeing him in the firelight, stared at him and said, 'This man also was with him.' But he denied it, saying, 'Woman, I do not know him'" (Luke 22:54–56). The conversation continued as did Peter's denial. There are a couple of other incidents in the life of Peter that were comparable. But a person can change! Much later, John records the conversation with Jesus at the end of his life. Jesus asks Peter if he truly loves him, a question that occurs three times. Peter affirms his love, it is accepted by Jesus, and Peter is given a strong affirmation that he will be a leader in the new Christian community. Jesus never gave up on Peter.

JUSTICE

Jesus is committed to truth in all of this word's various meanings, and he lived his life with a deep love that helped and healed all whom he met. Jesus was also keenly aware that true love, while given directly to individuals, takes the form of justice as one cares for groups of people and, indeed, for the whole human family. It is implied in several different verses in the Sermon on the Mount.

He speaks directly about the need to be an example as one who is in the process of influencing others to care for and maintain a safe and just society in which to live. For example, as Jesus describes the one who has become an integral part of the realm of God, he says, "You are the salt of the earth; but if salt has lost its taste, how can its saltiness be restored" (Matt 5:13). Again, Jesus says, "You are the light of the world. A city built on a hill cannot be hid. No one, after lighting a lamp, puts it under the bushel basket, but on the lampstand, and it gives light to all in the house. In the same way let your light shine before others, so that they may see your good works and give glory to your Father in heaven (Matt 5:14–16).

Jesus also cares for the formation of a just society by speaking about Jewish law, the way the Jewish people not only had personal values but had collective values that took the form of their law for a just and compassionate social order. Jesus says, "Do not think that I have come to abolish the law or the prophets; I have not come to abolish but to fulfill. For truly I tell you, until heaven and earth pass away, not one letter, not one stroke of a letter will pass away from the law until it is accomplished" (Matt 5:17–19). It is true that the law had to do with personal ethics, but it also had the purpose of teaching the values that should undergird the formation of a just society. It is a just society that has the capacity to create, build, and sustain a social order.

PEACE

It is from justice that peace emerges. Jesus even goes so far as to suggest that the way of the just society is to learn how to love one's enemies. Matthew records his teaching: "You have heard it said, 'You shall love your neighbor and hate your enemy.' But I say unto you, 'Love your enemies and pray for those who persecute you, so that you may be children of your Father in heaven; for he makes the sun rise on the evil and the good, and sends rain on the righteous and the unrighteous'" (Matt 5:43–45). Justice must be the foundation of the good society, creating a setting that honors all people, even as the sun and the rain meet the needs of all people. It is in such a society where conflicts are resolved by justice, and when there is justice, there is the presence of peace. Jesus says to his disciples, "Peace I leave with you, my peace I give unto you. I do not give to you as the world gives. Do not let your hearts be troubled, neither let them be afraid" (John 14:27).

It is, of course, difficult to summarize the values of Jesus. They are numerous and occasionally more directly illustrated in his actions than in his words. Fortunately, some of both his words and actions have been saved for succeeding generations of people who sense he is the teacher of the way that God would have us live. I have mentioned truth, love, and justice, and I would like to add a fourth word, peace, acknowledging that several others could be mentioned as well. Jesus was the truth and spoke the truth. He taught that unconditional love was the way to express the truth and way of life for those in the realm of God's presence in human life. And he taught that justice is the heartbeat of the good society. He also spoke about *peace as the outcome for those who follow God's will and way*, and it is the goal of the just society, giving people the security and resources to lead a good and productive society.

Jesus would have understood the meaning of peace in that it was at the heart of his Jewish faith. Our contemporary use of the word "peace" also has several variations of a common theme. Jesus would have been nurtured with the word *shalom* in Hebrew, which had some variations of meaning but essentially reflected the idea of wholeness and well-being. It was used with other terms, as it often is in English, such as "security" and even "prosperity." It was understood as both a gift of God and yet a value and quality of life for which we have some responsibility, not unlike love. In the Greek language, it had the meaning of the absence of strife among nations, a common meaning we give to the word. Both testaments underscore that peace is the gift of God, not unlike love, but a gift that must be cultivated, a task that is both personal and corporate. We seek peace of mind and peace among factions and nations.[9]

As Jesus used the word, he would have been influenced by the Hebrew meaning expressed in the Hebrew Bible, that sense of well-being and wholeness both within individuals and among corporate groups such as nations, states, and even local groups. It would have had at least three connotations: 1) having personal peace in that one has the right relation with oneself, 2) being at peace with others, and 3) being faithful, as a nation, to God's purpose.

Jesus in quoted as saying in a conversation with his disciples, using the metaphor of salt, "Salt is good; but if salt has lost its saltiness, how can you season it? Have salt in yourselves, and be at peace with one another" (Mark 9:50). In this teaching, Jesus is explaining that peace comes from

9. See the definition of "peace" in Achtemeier, *Harper's Bible Dictionary*, 766–77.

within, from the way we have been transformed by God. It is the product of God's influence in our lives. Luke speaks about the coming of one who will show us the way of peace: "to give light to those who sit in darkness and in the shadow of death, to guide our feet in the way of peace" (Luke 1:79). This promise is most direct in that it points to the way humans have a tendency to live in darkness, not knowing what is best, even with the threat of death. As Luke speaks about the coming of Jesus, he says "Glory to God in the highest heaven, and on earth peace to those whom he favors" (Luke 2:14). Luke notes in this saying that the influence of God (those whom God favors) is important in being at peace.

Paul, the disciple of Jesus who spread the word about Jesus and his teaching, speaks of peace both as our possession, because of the work of Jesus, and as our blessing, in that peace is the gift of God who is present with us. In Romans, his primary letter to new Christians in Rome, Paul says, "Therefore, since we are justified by faith, we have peace with God though our Lord Jesus Christ" (Rom 5:1). Jesus has removed all the barriers between God and the human family, although he does stress our need to endorse and claim this peace. In another letter, the one to the Galatians, he speaks of peace (and several other qualities) as the gift of God's presence in us as the Holy Spirit. "By contrast, the fruit of the Spirit is love, joy, peace, patience, kindness, generosity, faithfulness, gentleness, and self-control" (Gal 5:22). As these qualities become an integral part of our experience and an expression of our way of life, we do begin to truly find a quiet peace within us, an inner experience that is in short supply in our present world, and indeed, for those who live in nations where there is conflict and fear, where there are limited resources for adequate food and good health, and where there is regional and national governmental leadership that doesn't seem to think that personal peace, and in many cases national peace, are a high priority. We long to experience the saying of Jesus to his disciples, just prior to his absence with them: "Peace I leave with you, my peace I give unto you. I do not give to you as the world gives. Do not let your hearts be troubled, and do not let them be afraid" (John 14:27).

QUESTIONS FOR REFLECTION AND DISCUSSION

1. How often in your conversations with others on a given day do you have a hidden agenda or feel you would rather be somewhere else and doing something else?

2. Do you ever have the sense that God is with you, in your life and in your experience? If so, how would you describe it?
3. How important is having truth (avoiding falsehood and wisely and kindly saying what should be said) in every conversation and situation in your life?
4. How much do you think we can really know about the historical Jesus and discern his values in order to guide us?
5. How do you define our key words in this chapter (truth, love, justice, and peace)?

BOOKS TO CONSULT

1. Marcus J. Borg, *Jesus: Uncovering the Life, Teachings, and Relevance of a Religious Revolutionary*
2. C. Milo Connick, *Jesus: The Man, the Mission, and the Message*
3. John Dominic Crossan, *Jesus: A Revolutionary Biography*
4. Jaroslav Pelikan, *Jesus Through the Centuries*
5. N. T. Wright, *Jesus and the Victory of God*

SECTION THREE

To Do: Expressing the Mind and Heart of Jesus Across the Years

We have been using a relatively simple structure with three broad categories—to see, to be, and to do—identifying the flow of spiritual growth toward maturity. The simple formula has the problem of being just that, a simple and direct way of speaking about a very complex human experience. I would not want to communicate that the growth toward spiritual maturity is always simple, neat, and tidy; it is as complicated as our general growth and development. Spiritual growth is a very complex process, although occasionally made to sound too easy by enthusiastic preachers.

Interpreters of human growth and development have often used the concept of stages to describe our development. That is, we go through a series of stages, with each stage having a development task to complete in order to move on the next stage. James Fowler has used this frame of reference, one developed by Erik H. Erikson, to explain the categories or stages of growth in spiritual formation.[10] I will borrow from these two perceptive scholars as I speak about expressing the heart and mind of Jesus across the years.

The illustration below, using the circle with the spiritual center, will suggest that there are some healthy and some less-than-healthy ways in which we move toward a mature life and congruent spirituality. Note, as you look at the ways our spiritual center is both nurtured and influenced,

10. See Erikson, *Identity* and Fowler, *Stages of Faith*.

that there are both positive and negative influences as we seek to cultivate a deeper and more profound spirituality. We are influenced by our immediate context and usually a community of faith. Usually, these influences have a slightly different emphasis. Yet, these shaping influences allow for diversity, which is very positive. However, we may also, as we begin our spiritual journey, be in a support community that is filled with approaches that may be controlling rather than liberating, one that has the negative dimensions of being somewhat cultic, authoritarian, and exclusive. The best ways of cultivating a deeper spirituality have a focus on inner development, an appreciation of our uniqueness, and the transformation of the person, rather than imposing a single way of development that furthers the sectarian nature of the group in which one seeks guidance and support. It is also important to underline that each of us is a slightly different person who will thrive in a context that honors our identity and special needs.

Chapter Seven

The Mind and Heart of Jesus as Healer, Teacher, and Prophet

"Do not let your hearts be troubled. Believe in God, believe also in me. In my Father's house, there are many dwelling places. If it were not so, would I have told you that I go to prepare a place for you? And if I go and prepare a place for you, I will come again and will take you to myself, so that where I am, there you may be also. And you know the way to the place where I am going." Thomas said to him, "Lord, we do not know where you are going. How can we know the way?" Jesus said to him, "I am the way, and the truth, and the life."

—John 14:1–5

It is important to note that our spiritual growth will generally be shaped by the distinctiveness of the beliefs, traditions, and culture of the religion to which we are initially exposed. This exposure generally guides our pattern of spiritual development, although as we journey through life, there will be many other influences. I was initially guided in my growth by an enlightened evangelical orientation, one that stressed the reading of the Bible, daily prayer, active witness, and a supportive community. Across the years with an abundance of other influences, my orientation has matured while still valuing the earlier influences. For example, I have come to appreciate the deep and diverse patterns that exist within the Christian family and honor them. I have also been influenced and nurtured by other major religions such as Buddhism, a religion that has made deep spirituality the heart of being a Buddhist. And, of course, I have spent years studying the historical development of the Bible and given special attention to hermeneutics, carefully exploring the best ways to interpret the Bible.

Within the Christian church, I have been in a denomination or branch of the larger Christian family, the Reformed tradition, one that has placed a strong emphasis on the transcendence and sovereignty of God. Within this tradition, the need to encounter God through faith is stressed, and there is guidance about the process of receiving and maintaining the presence of God and the encouragement to engage in service. This pattern is present in different forms across the diversity of the Christian church; that is, we encounter God and follow in God's ways and engage in service. All of these experiences are undertaken not just out of our own capacities, but by being empowered by God's Spirit to be transformed, gain spiritual discernment, and receive the enabling power to follow the way of Jesus.

I have also been exposed to many nondenominational spiritual movements, which exist on the edge of nearly every major religion. Across the centuries, there have been many approaches to cultivate a spiritual life within the larger framework of religious life and faith, often only partially connected with a formal religion or a denominational branch of the Christian faith. These movements may have had an initial starting point within a formal religious structure, such as the spiritual way of the Jesuit movement within the Roman Catholic Church, but have now become somewhat independent and have grown out of a deep need for a profound spiritual center in order to live wisely and well in a perilous world.

Nearly every formal expression of religion has also had those members within it who have sensed a deep spiritual need, one not fully met within its formal structures. These movements often have a more countercultural frame of reference, sensing that the formal expression of the religion and the external culture in which they live do not have the capacity to meet their spiritual needs. A case can be made that part of the movement that emerged from the life and ministry of Jesus took this form. It was not an altogether gentle and easy transition from first-century Judaism to the new spiritual movement that was to become Christianity.

Most scholars of the beginning of Christianity have underlined that Jesus, as he began his public ministry, did not intend to start a new religion. In fact, as he left his work in the Galilee and traveled to a setting on the Jordan, he did not intend to move away from his Jewish heritage, but to consult with his cousin, John the Baptist, be baptized by him, and then be guided about next steps. Cousin John's ministry was not to start a new religion, but to deepen the faith of his Jewish constituency. Many people traveled from Jerusalem to the wilderness to hear him preach and to be baptized by him as the start of a deeper spiritual way of life.

John the Baptist spoke with Jesus about the goal of his ministry, and Jesus said that he wanted to assist John, and that his baptism was the starting point of his new life. John, expressing his deep humility, said to Jesus that he should be baptized by Jesus who already had a deep and profound spiritual life. Jesus affirmed the ministry of his cousin John, left the region of the Jordan River, and went to a wilderness area on retreat in order to prepare himself for his God-given calling as healer, teacher, and prophet.

What we observe about the life of Jesus is a pattern that is not uncommon, that is, to sense that his way of life as a carpenter, while important work, was not his true calling. His true calling, by the grace of God, was to guide his people in Israel-Palestine to a deeper spiritual path, one filled with healing, teaching, and bold action to challenge the Jewish spiritual leaders to create a more just and peaceful setting. He then went into the wilderness to prepare himself for his life mission and to learn how to overcome those human temptations that would prevent him from fulfilling his calling.

THE CONTEXT

Jesus left the wilderness, returned to his home region in the Galilee, and began his public ministry. Matthew, in his Gospel, summarized this period in the life of Jesus:

> Jesus went throughout Galilee, teaching in their synagogues and proclaiming the good news of the kingdom and curing every disease and every sickness among the people. So, his fame spread throughout all Syria, and they brought to him all the sick, those who were afflicted with various diseases and pains, demoniacs, epileptics, and paralytics, and he cured them. And great crowds followed him from Galilee, the Decapolis, Jerusalem, Judea, and from beyond the Jordan. (Matt 4:23–25)

Jesus began his work in his home region of Galilee, a vast area in the northern section of Israel-Palestine. We learn, as we read the Gospels about the early portion of his ministry, that he was remarkably busy healing, teaching, preaching, and proclaiming the need for a just society that would give the people a safe haven in which to live, work, have children, and move through their lives with a good measure of peace and fulfillment.

As I read about his life in this period, I realize why his presence and message was so attractive to the people in the Galilee and beyond to other parts of the country. Being from this part of Israel-Palestine, he was able to speak clearly and simply with them, understand and listen to them, and then act directly to meet their needs. There were several issues and concerns he faced during these two or more years of his public ministry.[1] He was so focused and committed to caring for the people, and he addressed all aspects of their lives, what they believed, their health, their challenges, and the patterns of their lives in a relatively complex cultural setting.

As I begin this description of this time in the life of Jesus, I am aware that we lack some information about the way Jesus lived within his home region. We do know that he traveled to this region, following his baptism, and we have a few good reports of his activity and the content of his teaching in the Gospels, but there were no filmed interviews of him or manuscripts that he composed.[2] But, thankfully, we do have the essential information from the Gospels, and, of course, several centuries of commentary by excellent scholars of his life and teaching.

I want to reflect on the content of his teaching and the values of his life that emerge as we read about his public ministry in the Gospels.[3] How might they be perceived and embraced and influence our lives? I want to list just a few issues, categories, and topics that were integral to his teaching and ministry and then classify these topics in terms of their possible influence on our lives. The overarching category I want to use to understand the way he taught his followers to be spiritual was *to open one's heart to the reign of God*. In a broad sense, this notion of receiving God's reign would help them find a path that would lead them to ways of being more mature, wise, informed, and at peace. The heart of his teaching about being deeply spiritual was to become a citizen of the kingdom of God and embrace the reign of God in one's life. Receiving God's reign in one's life would empower his followers to cultivate a mature life, one filled with integrity, peace, and purpose. Jesus started with this foundational goal as he taught all those whom he met who longed for answers that would give them a healthy, peaceful, and engaged life.

1. The precise length of time of the public ministry of Jesus is a bit hard to determine, although the generally accepted time of nearly three years may be as accurate as we can be, although his time in public ministry may have been a bit shorter.

2. We do have the results of an oral tradition, one that preserved some of his teaching and chronicled his travels.

3. The literature on this subject is extensive!

At that time, there were many who were ill or disfigured and had no way to deal with these limitations. There were not doctors with the specialty needed, no modern medicine, and few places to seek help.

JESUS AS HEALER

So, one of the greatest needs in the setting of Israel-Palestine as Jesus began his ministry was to help and heal people who had a mixture of diseases. There was a variety of disorders that were physical in nature and were addressed by Jesus: fever, leprosy, paralysis, intellectual disability, atrophy, hemorrhages, deafness and speech impediment, blindness, epilepsy, general infirmity, dropsy, and even, in two settings, a severed ear. There are, of course, a number of questions regarding whether and how Jesus dealt with this array of physical ailments. The biblical record affirms that Jesus had deep empathy for those who were ill and that he healed the vast majority of those who were brought to him or came directly to him. More than a hundred are recorded in the Gospels, and almost all were healed.[4]

As he began his ministry in the region of Galilee, he was immediately asked for help in healing those who were ill. Those who came to him or were brought to him had a range of illnesses; some were defined as needing exorcisms (casting out demons), healing of illness such as leprosy or a paralysis, and even resuscitation of those thought to be dead. A quite dramatic exorcism happened in the region of Gerasa, a setting Jesus did not visit frequently. It raises several questions, although the outcome of healing was clearly the goal.[5] The questions have to do with why Jesus was in the region of Gerasa, not his usual place of ministry, with the very strange case of the Gerasene demoniac with the casting out of the demons into pigs, and with the pigs running into the lake to be drowned. There may be a "cause-effect" explanation, with the pigs being afraid of what might have happened and stampeding into the water. This sort of event is very rare, and it might cause the reader to wonder whether the event actually occurred. Was there a natural occurrence that scared the pigs and caused them to stampede? The events described were perhaps more the result of being truly impressed

4. It is interesting that not all of the groupings of Christians and their leaders have focused on this aspect of the ministry of Jesus. Of course, the Christian Science movement is the exception. I personally find it remarkable that Jesus had the wisdom, patience, and obviously some power to heal and help so many.

5. Matt 8:28–34.

by what did occur, the healing of a very sick man, rather than providing a precise explanation of all that occurred.

In terms of the larger question regarding the healing power of Jesus, one may want to factor in the presence of a prescientific understanding of unusual events in the time of Jesus. To describe an event that is unusual then or now, the one who provides the explanation deals with the facts of a specific event, but also calls upon an understanding of reality in order to report on the event and stress its importance. One might say that the doctor healed a person in a remarkable way, using the best remedies of modern science. Another person, observing the healing, might say that God was active in the healing process. I do accept that Jesus truly healed many of these ill people, doing God's work, and gave them encouragement and peace of mind that aided their healing.

The remarkable ministry of healing by Jesus has been understood in a variety of ways:

1. Affirm the truth of the report literally.
2. Maintain that the world has changed; for example, demons do not exist and are not the cause of illness. There are scientific explanations.
3. Say that the events occurred, but have been misinterpreted; demon possession is the first-century equivalent of mental illness.
4. Accept that the question remains an unsolved problem and affirm that modern scholarship sheds light.
5. See the stories as pious explanations in a pre-scientific era.[6]

I personally tend to view these healings and many of the other miraculous occurrences that are described in the Bible as remarkable and reported on honestly from the worldview that was present in the time it happened. There was the use of prescientific categories of explanation available in that era. Yet there may have been occurrences that cannot easily and fully be explained by saying that they were natural occurrences described at that time by the use of prescientific categories. In the Christian tradition, the resurrection, central to the Christian faith, is often described as and thought to be a miracle, although it too has been explained in natural ways.

What may more easily earn the right to be described as miraculous is the care, patience, actions, insight, and comforting presence of Jesus. He had remarkable insight, empathy, and compassion for those who suffered

6. See the account of Jesus as healer in Connick, *Jesus*, 266–80.

and who had little hope that they would be healed. His ministry to them, giving them his time, attention, and care, remain a model for all those who dare to say that they want to "follow Jesus," yet without the assumption that they can perform "miracles."

JESUS AS TEACHER

There is little diversity of opinion on whether Jesus was a great teacher. In general, even if one does not fully accept all that he taught, he is nearly always acknowledged to be a marvelous teacher, perhaps the greatest teacher of all time. He not only taught well, but he taught about subjects that are of vital importance to the welfare of most humans. He taught about meaning and purpose, about love and compassion, about danger and death, and then he modeled much of the great wisdom he taught in his remarkable life and courageous death. He was a model rabbi. It is not possible in this brief section to do justice to his teaching, but I do want to highlight some of the subjects of his teaching, his way of teaching, and the influence of his teaching.

A distinctive feature of the teaching of Jesus was that he often taught in a way that encouraged the listener to reflect on what is being said, rather than merely jotting down the subject of the teaching and putting it in a file or the bottom drawer. The teaching of Jesus was engaging, inviting the listener and reader to ponder and reflect and, in many cases, to search one's conscience or find ways to implement the lesson of the teaching.

One primary way that Jesus accomplished the goal of engaging the reader was the use of the parable, a form of teaching that places a great truth within a story, and in the case of Jesus, a spiritual story, one that most often uses a comparison. The parable is a profound simile or metaphor, a statement and comparison of likeness. Often, as he taught, he would begin the comparison with an "I am": "I am the good shepherd," "I am the door," or "I am the way."[7] On occasion, the parable may move toward a story, as in the case of the good Samaritan (Luke 10:30–37).

As Jesus taught in these creative ways, he used a method that was not uncommon in his time, one that was tangible and had a definite purpose. He wanted to catch the attention of his listeners and teach them a lesson and invite them to think about very important issues. In some cases, the meaning of the parable might have been a bit hard to discern, causing the

7. Connick, *Jesus*, 202–36.

listener to think in some depth about a concern or attitude. In most cases, the parable was a method to communicate a truth, an invitation to believe, or even a way to confuse and perplex the listener so that the person would reflect on its deep meaning.

The followers of Jesus found them stimulating and an attractive way to think about an important issue or pattern of belief. They were a stimulus to encourage, inspire, and act in accord with the values of their faith. In particular, they often became the means of teaching about the deepest truth of all, that God reigns and invites the human family to receive the presence of God into their lives. Those in the kingdom are then asked to advance the reign kingdom of God.[8] God does reign, and in the language of Jesus, God reigns in the following ways:

1. By being near and active in transforming our lives
2. By reassuring us that the rule of God is coming and sure
3. By being inclusive, with the arms of love wrapping around all of humankind
4. By teaching a way of life that may be costly and demanding
5. By teaching that this way of life is of great value
6. By teaching that this way of God's rule will prevail[9]

Jesus often taught these values with the use of the creative parable, but he also taught in a more direct way with the sermon. I want to note that the use of the word sermon may be an accurate way of describing some of the teaching of Jesus, but it might suggest that he spoke too long on irrelevant issues; it happens in some churches. Yet, as far as we can tell with the records we have, his sermons were not too long or on subjects of little interest. Of course, what we have are not word-for-word accounts of all he said and taught. What we do have are remarkable accounts of his sermons, initially repeating what he taught in a small group by the spoken word. It was a nonliterate culture, and initially there were only the spoken accounts of his teaching. Much of what Jesus taught was remembered because it was often repeated for the benefit of others. It was an oral culture that

8. The use of the word kingdom is somewhat problematic in that it is clearly a reference to a masculine ruler and, of course, in the time of Jesus and perhaps across history, many rulers have been masculine. It is important to note that we understand God as a loving and guiding ruler, without a specific gender, but one who loves and guides as a dear and powerful parent and ruler.

9. See Connick, *Jesus*, 236.

had perfected the art of sharing with others in an oral way what was said in important gatherings. Much of what Jesus said in his teaching and preaching has been preserved for us, passing from an oral form to a written form over a period of several decades.

The Bibles we use have two major sections that preserved what he said in summary form, one called the Sermon on the Mount, found in Matthew 5–7, and one called the Sermon on the Plain (Luke 6:20–49).[10] The titles of these sections of Scripture might suggest that they were spoken at one time, but in fact they are collections of "talks," put together as an organized summary of the teaching of Jesus.

JESUS AS PROPHET

Earlier, we reviewed in outline form the content of the Sermon on the Mount in chapters 5 through 7 in Matthew's Gospel. This material is profound and life-giving! But, fortunately, there was another account, although much shorter, in the Gospel of Luke called the Sermon on the Plain. There is some overlap in the two accounts, although the one in the Gospel of Luke is shorter and has slightly different content and tone. In Matthew's version, we do see clearly what it means to understand and endorse the reign of God. Luke's version is shorter and describes the teaching of Jesus in a way that may easily be understood by the non-Jewish reader.

The version of the "sermon" in Luke begins with beatitudes, although a shorter version than in Matthew, and Luke adds "woes" at the end of the blessings. The authors of Matthew and Luke had slightly different resources and purposes, yet both were sensitive to their possible and respective readers. Luke's version of the beatitudes, like Matthew's, starts with "Blessed are the poor, for yours is the kingdom of God" (Luke 6:20) in order to be inclusive, wanting the poor to know of God's blessing. Luke was not Jewish, and he writes for those not altogether familiar with Jewish history. He aims directly at those who are needy and suffering, reassuring them that they are not forgotten by God. The poor are able to experience the presence of God with the fullness of God's blessings, just as much and as easily as those with some wealth and a Jewish heritage. The second beatitude follows in kind: "Blessed are you who are hungry, for you shall be filled; and blessed are you who weep now for you will laugh" (6:21). Luke is reassuring his readers

10. These accounts do not contain all of what he taught and said, but they do contain his central message.

that God's love is abundant and cares for those who are poor, hungry, and sad; God's love is present for all those who are neglected and whose suffering is very real. In fact, it is there even "when people hate you, when they exclude you, and when they revile you and defame you" (when they show prejudice and punish you) (6:22). God's love is there for the minorities who are excluded from the blessings and full inclusion of the mainline culture.

Luke clearly states that those who are left out and treated poorly shall be blessed by God, as the prophets were when they spoke out against the injustice perpetrated by the majority culture. And woe to those who are rich, who have prestige, power, and material blessings, and who laugh in a condescending way at those in need. History tells us that their time of suffering will come and that justice will be done (Luke 6:22–26). These teachings, at times a bit difficult to interpret, do place Jesus in the important role of prophet.

There have been times across history when Jesus has been viewed almost exclusively as just helping little children (and he does), but this view needs to supplemented with the reality that Jesus was a courageous prophet, standing tall and speaking directly to the issues of injustice and being a powerful and supportive voice for the poor and the disenfranchised (women, children, and minorities).

JESUS AS PASTOR AND PRIEST

In Luke, Jesus is described as one who heals and has compassion and one who speaks and acts as the prophet, seeking to overcome the injustice that contributes to human suffering. Matthew also records these elements of the mission of Jesus in his account, although he does tend to emphasize that Jesus is the great teacher. Luke does as well in his account of the Sermon on the Plain as he lists and describes the subjects about which Jesus teaches. Luke addresses several subjects, many of which emphasize that the mission of Jesus is to comfort those who are troubled. The teaching is filled with great insight and wisdom, guiding the troubled soul.

In the account in Luke, Jesus speaks to two of the most disconcerting problems we have as we go through a day, a week, a month, and a year. Problem one is that no matter how skilled we are in human relationships, we occasionally will have those who, for a variety of reasons, become our enemy, those who may not like or support us, or those who engage in activities that go against our values and points of view. What does Jesus teach us about how to deal with those who become "our enemies"? He is clear: "Love your enemies, do good to those who hate you, bless those who curse you, pray for those who abuse you. If anyone strikes you on the cheek, offer the other also; and from anyone who takes away your coat do not withhold even your shirt. Give to everyone who begs from you; and if anyone takes away your goods, do not ask for them again. Do to others as you would have them do to you" (Luke 6:27–31).

These teachings of Jesus have been difficult for Christians to follow, when and since he spoke them. Books on these profound sayings of Jesus fill libraries, and pastors and scholars continue to explain how these teachings would improve the human condition if they were practiced. It is not all that easy to summarize what has been spoken and written, but there has been a general understanding by most reputable interpreters. It is that when we intentionally and carefully identify with those who may be called our "enemy," we *have deep empathy for them* and try to understand what contributed to how this offensive person became one who harms others. We attempt to see them not only as needing our resistance to their behavior, but also as those who have been conditioned to harm. Then we go to them, understanding and caring about the way they have been shaped and influenced in negative ways. We understand them as being conditioned to resort to willful evil to solve their problems and as needing understanding and forgiveness. We respond to them in two ways:

1. We wisely resist the wrong behavior in an understanding and wise way; the person feels understood and cared for in the sense of being in the presence of those who want what is best for them.
2. We use a nonaggressive, clear, and firm strategy of deep empathy to change their behavior. It is how God comes to us, heals us, and points us to new and compassionate ways to deal with conflict and differences.

Luke goes directly to another human tendency that has the potential to just make things worse; it is the tendency to harshly judge others. Again, Luke records that Jesus was very direct that judging others will make things worse by inviting harsh judgment in return. "Do not judge, and you will not be judged; do not condemn, and you will not be condemned. Forgive, and you will be forgiven; give, and it will be given to you. A good measure, pressed down, shaken together, running over, will be put into your lap; for the measure you give will be the measure you get back" (Luke 6:37–38). In fact, if you give generously to others, if you receive them unconditionally and affirm them, you will be treated in the same way, establishing a trusting and fulfilling friendship. Jesus adds a short parable to further explain his views on the negative impact of harsh and unfair judgment of others. "Why do you see the speck in your neighbor's eye, but do not notice the log in your own eye? Or how can you say to your neighbor, 'Friend, let me take out the speck in your eye when you yourself do not see the log in your own eye. You hypocrite, first take the log out of your own eye, and then you will see clearly to take the speck out of your neighbor's eye'" (Luke 6:41–42). It is when we are humble, acknowledging our own limitations, and approach our neighbor with a sincere desire to be helpful, rather than needing to feel superior and have power over others, that true love is given and received.

Luke goes on to say to say that appropriate care and concern is expressed as we nurture a foundation based on love and truth. It is like a fig tree that provides good fruit. The "figs are gathered not from thorns, nor are grapes picked from a bramble bush. The good person out of the good treasure of the heart produces good, and the evil person out of the evil treasure produces evil; for it is out of the abundance of the heart that the mouth speaks" (Luke 6:44–45). How often it is that we speak an unkind word or make an unfair judgment of another, and when we do, we harm a life-giving friendship and hurt the one we claim to love. There is nothing vague about this wise teaching of Jesus, so important in all human relationships.

He goes on to explain that it has to do with foundations. It is like building a house on a strong foundation, and when the flood comes, the house remains steady and firm. But if we build a house without a solid foundation and the river bursts against it, the house will collapse and be ruined. So it is with our lives: if we build a foundation in our relationships based on love and truth, then when trouble comes and there is misunderstanding, the relationship can be restored easily; but if we have been dishonest and it is discovered by our friend, the relationship will be seriously damaged.

A WAY OF LIFE

Luke continues to tell the story of Jesus in a way that helps us understand how we should live our lives. I have read and reread the account of the life and teaching of Jesus in Luke's Gospel, and I never fail to be inspired, humbled, and then motivated and energized to model my life and my ethical values on the patterns of life and values that filled the life of Jesus. At times,

I even wish that I could have been one of his disciples who saw him teach the truth and love others in such a marvelous way. Yet I remain profoundly grateful that we have the accounts of his life in the Gospels. While it is true that the writers of the Gospels were not critical historians, we nevertheless get an accurate and inspiring account, perhaps of even more value than a straightforward historical narrative because the authors—Matthew, Mark, Luke, and John—spoke with an eye on accuracy to be sure, but also with the motivation to communicate deep values, inspiring love, bold action, and the pathway to a life of profound meaning and purpose. They point us in a profound way to how to follow Jesus in a complex environment. They point to the identity and calling of Jesus. A brief summary may be helpful.

THE IDENTITY AND ROLES OF JESUS

What comes to mind initially as one reads the Gospels and consults with the many interpreters is that the life and teaching of Jesus may be understood in several ways as he undertook his mission.

1. As a teacher: He taught with great wisdom, courage, and desire to expand and deepen the understanding of those he taught; his words healed, inspired, motivated, and changed the world. He is often thought of as the world's greatest teacher of ethics and the spiritual life.
2. As a healer: Whenever and wherever he went, he healed people. In many cases there were those who had physical diseases, those born with an infirmity, a paralysis, and the incapacity to move with ease. He also healed those with emotional illness, those confused about life, and those without the capacity to manage hardship in many of its forms.
3. As a prophet: He speaks the truth and challenges all forms of discrimination as one who points to a better future for a just and peaceful social order, one who envisions a better life for all who are victims of discrimination, and one who acts boldly to improve the life of those who suffer from injustice.
4. As a pastor and priest: He practiced what he taught and preached by going to the places where those who struggle and suffer are located, talking with them, giving them insight and hope, and helping to heal their physical and psychological ailments.

5. As Savior: He is one who came to remove the barriers between God and the human family, understood differently in various religious settings, but with the primary goal of helping pilgrims to find a true and gratifying relationship of people to God. He "saved" them from being lost and frustrated, and showed them the way to the loving heart of God.
6. As Lord: This is a term that often points directly to divinity, and Jesus has been understood in the Christian faith as being "a Lord" in the divine Trinity of Father, Son, and Holy Spirit. But he emancipated rather than imprisoned, and set people free to be.

SUBJECTS HE TAUGHT AND LIVED AND INVITED PEOPLE TO ENDORSE

1. The purpose of life is to love God and one's neighbor.
2. The tangible ethical values that are inherent in the love commandment and that should be practiced in one's life.
3. The way to be related to and live in harmony with God, resulting in a life of peace, purpose, and guidance.
4. The way to "practice the presence"[11] of God and undertake the spiritual life.
5. The way to be God's disciple and do good in the world.

THE VALUES THAT CHARACTERIZED HIS LIFE AND ARE IMPLICIT IN HIS LIFE AND TEACHING

1. Unconditional love, to be practiced in one's daily life and understood as the way God cares for humans
2. Deep and thoughtful faith to understand the reigning presence of God (kingdom of God) in one's life and seek to follow God's will, and so live with integrity

11. Lawrence, *Practice of the Presence.*

3. Inspiring and motivating hope that life can be managed with a positive outlook because of God's presence and great love
4. Nurturing and sustaining peace of mind because of God's love and empowering presence
5. Bold and direct challenges to that which harms all humans and the earth's atmosphere, to be prophetic especially for those who live in poverty and are the victims of injustice
6. The pursuit, with wisdom and commitment, of the mission to create a just society that heals and brings peace
7. Empathy and kind actions that heal the sick and comfort the perplexed, the challenged, and those with deep needs
8. The pursuit of emancipating freedom for all those who suffer from poverty and injustice
9. Emancipation from careless religious thought and practice and seeking an informed faith and trustworthy guidance to discover insights and directions for a mature life based on truth
10. Commitment to being a world citizen, helping to reshape governments and institutions that do not honor human rights or seek the welfare of their citizens

QUESTIONS FOR REFLECTION AND DISCUSSION

1. How have you been influenced by your family, your place of residence in your early life, and your schooling?
2. Do you have a set of foundational values, and if so, what are they?
3. How do these values guide you day to day as you go through life?
4. How do you understand the meaning of your life? Would you ever use the concepts of calling or vocation in describing your journey through life?
5. How has your religion, and Christianity in particular, been formative in shaping your life?

BOOKS TO CONSULT

1. Diana Butler Bass, *Grounded: Finding God in the World—A Spiritual Revolution*
2. Ilia Delio, *Making All Things New: Catholicity, Cosmology, and Consciousness*
3. Phillip J. Newell, *Listening to the Heartbeat of God: A Celtic Spirituality*
4. David Richo, *How to Be an Adult: A Handbook on Psychological and Spiritual Integration*
5. Richard Rohr, *The Universal Christ: How a Forgotten Reality Can Change Everything We See, Hope for, and Believe*

Chapter Eight

The Mind and Heart of Jesus in a Demanding and Perilous World

Again, he began to teach beside the sea. Such a very large crowd gathered around him that he got into a boat on the sea and sat there, while the whole crowd was beside the sea on the land. He began to teach them many things in parables, and in his teaching, he said to them: "Listen! A sower went out to sow. And as he sowed, some seeds fell on the path and the birds came and ate it up. Another seed fell on rocky ground where it did not have much soil, and it sprang up quickly, since it had no depth of soil. And when the sun rose, it was scorched, and since it had no root, it withered away. Another seed fell among thorns, and the thorns grew up and choked it, and it yielded no grain. Other seeds feel into good soil and brought forth grain, growing up and increasing and yielding thirty and sixty and hundredfold." And he said, "Let anyone with ears to hear listen."

—Mark 4:1–9

INTRODUCTION: MEETING HUMAN NEED

Jesus taught at a time in history when there were no supermarkets and probably only a few open markets that certainly didn't look like our grocery stores. It may not have been uncommon for him to tell a story about farming and the need for food. His listeners could easily identify with planting a crop, and he could usually catch the attention of his followers with his metaphor about farmers planting seeds and having good crops that would feed the people.

On one occasion, he began to explain to his disciples that the message of God's love and care for the human family will not always be understood and received as it is taught by the religious leaders. Their message may have been too abstract and vague, focused more on who has authority to determine government structures and correct beliefs. Even the use of religious language may have slightly turned them off and caused them to mumble, "I have heard that before." He said that to teach in parables might help the people to understand in a better way (Mark 4:10–20).

Jesus knew he could catch their attention with a story, a method he used often in his ministry. He loved metaphors that connected with the everyday life of those who came to listen. In one story, he used the illustration of the farmer who plants seeds in order to have good crops that will feed hungry people. As a teacher with gifts, experience, and a keen awareness of human needs, he sensed that his listeners would more likely respond to a parable or a story, which would help them hear the message of God's love.

I have had a similar experience as I taught several years in three small universities and often in churches. I thought I was a modestly good teacher, but I discovered over several decades of teaching that not every student will listen with great care, be eager to learn, and then use the information and insight of the class to manage the demands of life and to flourish. In fact, it was a challenge to get students to listen, learn, and use their new knowledge in constructive ways. In these endeavors, I gained insight and encouragement from Jesus, whose stories caught the attention of the people with whom he spoke. I often used a story as I began the class.

Jesus was the great teacher and he taught his disciples how to teach, that is, how to *plants seeds* that would grow and have the capacity to empower people to move into maturity and manage life in a constructive and fulfilling way. He underlined that there will be those who listen and receive the full value of the seeds of love and truth and then blossom. Yet he was also realistic and said that there will be some passive listeners and those who even reject his message. Those who plant "seeds" need to understand that the seed must fall on fertile soil for it to grow into a healthy plant or a mature person. Jesus, using this comparison, teaches us how to plant our seeds in good soil so there will be a healthy plant, producing good fruit, a beautiful flower, and a mature person; it depends on the nature of the soil.

In his remarkably gifted way, he says that there may be four different kinds of surface (soil) on which the seeds will be sown, or four different kinds of settings or types of soil in which people may plant the seeds of love and truth, hoping that listeners will grow into more mature and responsible adults.

TYPES OF SOIL

Jesus first mentions that a farmer may go out to plant seeds for a crop, but as the farmer walks on the path to garden, some of the seeds may fall from his basket on the path. These seeds will not likely grow because the path has a hard surface; the seeds will not produce a good crop because they fell on poor soil. Second, Jesus notes that the farmer's seeds will not always grow because there may be rocks in the soil, making the soil less fertile. Third, he notes that as the seeds remain on the surface of the hardened soil, birds will come and eat the seeds. Fourth, Jesus says that many of the seeds will not grow because they were planted in the midst of thorns, and as the thorns grow, they take over and "choke" the good seeds. Hardened and rocky soil, hungry birds, and dangerous thorns are a challenge as we make our way in life and learn how to plant the seeds of love and justice.

In my years of teaching, I have scattered a few seeds on hard and rocky surfaces, ones where thorns were present and where birds had come and eaten the seeds. I even scattered a few of them on the path that leads to the garden rather than in the rich soil of the garden. As I look back on how I planted my seeds, I did it reasonably well, but I wish that I had been more careful on a few occasions when I was careless in my planting. I certainly did want my students to grow and develop, but looking back, I realize that some of my seeds of wisdom fell on hardened soil, among the rocks, and where there were thorns on the bushes. The birds had a good meal, but my students went away hungry for knowledge.

It is no secret that we all live in regions where there is a variety of poor soils. As we engage in the *planting of our seeds*, there is the risk that some of the seeds will fall on the hardened path, the rocky soil, and too close to thorns that fill our culture. These pathways may appear attractive at first glance, but they do not empower growth toward wholeness and a responsible life. If we plant carelessly and in the wrong place, we will discover that a few of our seeds did not go deeply into good soil, but remained on top of the ground and were eaten by birds. I learned that a form of this story occasionally occurs in an academic setting where the pathway to knowledge has hardened soil, where there are plenty of birds to "eat the seeds" with good arguments, and even some distracting bushes with thorns. I soon realized that as I taught, I needed for there to be good soil for the students to learn and good ways to share knowledge and speak the truth.

Jesus speaks in his story about the reality that seeds may not grow into healthy plants if the garden is filled with rocks and plants with thorns. As a teacher at the university level, when I went about teaching in a classroom, I occasionally discovered that the soil was hardened, full of rocks, and there were plants with thorns. In short, the students were not ready or able to learn. The blackboards may have been filled with items discussed in the last class that used the room. Or the temperature of the room was too warm and students began to doze. It was also the case that there was often a group of students who sat in the back, used their electronic devises, and failed to listen or engage in conversation. I had a good measure of patience for these students, knowing that many of them were preoccupied with concerns that may have been more important than my "seeds," but I did work diligently to catch their attention with more than just a few random seeds that fell on rocky soil in which plants with thorns were present. There were times when I used "parables," and sure enough, students paid attention and learned. Yes, there were days when I wasn't sufficiently prepared, or perhaps I was preoccupied with my personal concerns, and the classroom was not arranged for good learning. Not unlike Jesus, I soon learned the reality that not every student will be prepared to learn every day, in part because of my failure to be well prepared and in part because of external circumstances. I know that their desire to gain knowledge and wisdom must be met by diligent planning and good storytelling.

Jesus knew that there were hindrances to good learning, and he worked diligently to find settings in which the best environment for learning was present. Yet, he also had to teach in environments that may not have been ideal, and he was still able even to use those settings to illustrate the truths that he carefully explained. There is the story of him teaching from a boat because those who came to listen to him had filled the shore. He was a creative teacher and taught from a boat and illustrated his message from the setting. I have tried to learn from his method of teaching, knowing that there are settings or "fields" of learning that make it difficult for students to learn. But I also learned from Jesus that it was still possible to use the setting to illustrate an important point, one in which students are motivated to learn. He was able to use nearly every setting to teach the important lessons of life.

I remember two situations where I visited schools in Africa, ones in which the classrooms were housed in a limited structure with a leaky roof, a setting without blackboards and where there were no chairs or desks for the nearly sixty students. The ground floor was hardened soil, and the students sat on this floor. I was amazed that the young children paid attention, and that the teacher was able to keep the students' concentration and focus. Good learning did take place, largely because of the teacher's remarkable spirit and the excellent preparation. Unfortunately, as well as they did with what they had, the students did not always learn in a comprehensive way. The setting for the learning was far from ideal. There was not enough good soil for the students to receive an education that would prepare them to live wisely and well in a complex and even dangerous society. Some of the students were unable to go beyond what we call "middle school," and as I discerned the needs of the town and the country, I hoped that one day there would be the resources to provide a solid and advanced education for these students. I celebrated my denomination's vision and work in such difficult settings. I also remembered the teaching of Jesus that "other seeds fell into good soil and brought forth grain."

As it sometimes happens, I was invited to stay and help, but it was just not possible for me to shift the focus of my work and my family's life to help the school and the region of central Africa. For me, the "rocks and thorns" were not just in the soil and setting of the school, but in the complexity of shifting one's life to lend a hand in a foreign setting. In one of these situations, they were anticipating the start of a seminary, training people who would be prepared to teach the good news of God's love. It was a setting with great vision, remarkable faith, and life-giving hope. The team of mission workers did the very best they could, and I was deeply moved by the need and the wonderful people addressing the need, but knew that my journey was in another location. As I left, I was so proud that my denomination, the Presbyterian Church (USA), had made this profound need for education a high priority.

ADDRESSING THE EDUCATIONAL NEEDS IN A PERILOUS WORLD

There is the profound need, nearly worldwide, for basic education that will help students learn what is needed for living well from day to day across their span of life. There is also the need for more specialized education that will enable students to learn how to live carefully in a threatening context. They must learn how to read, write, do basic mathematics, and be efficient in the use of computers and other learning devices. But they also need to learn how to cope with the severe dangers in their setting. In many parts of the world, there is the need for an educational system that will inform students how to live with care and wisdom in a threatening world. This need is especially important in developing countries where the governments may be unstable and have limited resources for a good system of education. Their unique environment and safety needs will require a comprehensive educational system, developed across time as funds and good teachers are available. It needs to be one that is deeply rooted in their culture and history and that takes into account the threats to the safety of the citizens of the country. All of the questions are present for those in charge of education in settings such as Gaza or Ukraine.

At this point, I want to make the case that in many settings there is a need to teach ethics and cultivate a way of life with purpose and meaning. It is often the case that the predominant religious outlook in the students' setting will be a good resource to help students develop an ethical and spiritual dimension in their life. Of course, this dimension of life may be taught in regional temples and churches, and there is the risk that teaching "religion" in the public schools may be driven by narrow, cultic, and exclusive views. Yet religion is a very important dimension in one's personal life, and it often has a profound influence in most countries. Religion often has a place in the lives of students, and if it is taught in a way that respects alternative traditions, it will give students an appreciation of an informed and reformed religious outlook, one that respects the views of others, and a context in which to deal with ethical concerns in a perilous world filled with conflict.[1]

I have found in my study of the great religions of the world, and in particular within the life and teaching of Jesus, that there is some direction for the human family about how to address and manage the educational needs in today's world. More specifically, I want to reflect on how we as individuals might become better prepared to live wisely in our threatened and perilous world. Initially, I am suggesting that one way to be prepared is to increase our knowledge about the values that guided Jesus in his roles as a healer, teacher, and prophet. He, too, lived in perilous world. How did he manage his life and focus his mission in a demanding and dangerous

1. See my book entitled *Exploring the Spirituality of the World Religions.*

world? And within my frame of reference, I have found that there are important lessons to learn from Jesus about how to cope with threats and find resources with which to manage our lives in our present settings.

One place to start is to lift up a saying that has captured the attention of people across the centuries in different countries and cultures. It is a saying of Jesus, but it has also been present as a starting point and frame of reference for learning how to live in several cultures of the world. It is called the Golden Rule, a short statement, yet one that is foundational and has the capacity to guide all of us. It is one that is present in several countries, cultures, and religions.

Buddhism: Hurt not others with that which pains yourself.

Hinduism: Treat others as you would yourself want to be treated.

Islam: Do unto all men (people) as you would wish to have done to you.

Judaism: What you yourself hate, do to no man (person).

Native American: Live in harmony, for we are all related.

Sacred Earth: Do as you will, as long as you harm no one.

Christianity: Do unto others as you would have them do unto you.[2]

Few would argue with the wisdom of these sayings, but unfortunately, the sayings are not specific and have been focused almost exclusively on the individual. There is a deep need to expand their meaning and relevance for current policies and programs in many regions and countries. I want to speak to the ways that Jesus epitomized the undergirding ethical norm of the Golden Rule and suggest that it contains in embryonic form the ethics for living and educating in a demanding and perilous world. How might we learn to live in a dangerous world guided by the ethical norms that are present in the Golden Rule? And then how do we expand these norms and make them germane to regions and countries with few resources and unstable leadership? How might the life and teachings of Jesus be applied to the extraordinary challenges of our time? Might the revolutionary teaching of Jesus give us some guidance, affirming the norm of loving all people?

One good place to start looking for an answer is to seek clarity about his identity, shaped as it was by Jewish teaching and practice in his time. Our records do give us some clues. For example, he was born and raised

2. I have this list among my notes, though I am unsure of its origin. I may have compiled it from various sources for a presentation or a class in world religions.

in a Jewish home, with an extraordinary mother and a reputable and responsible father. He likely worked with his father as a carpenter well into his adult life.

He was rooted in his Jewish faith, and in a limited way, he may have also been exposed to Greek and Roman thought. The Romans were the ruling power, and the Greek language was spoken in public life. Our limited historical records indicate that at some point in his adult life, Jesus sensed a call to become a teacher and prophet.

We do have limited information about this choice, yet his values soon become apparent as we observe how he lived and what he taught. The record is also relatively clear about the influence of John the Baptist on Jesus, who sensed a clear calling after the time with his cousin John. Jesus left John and continued his preparation for his calling in the wilderness region near the Dead Sea. He emerged from these experiences better prepared to assume his ordained role as a teacher and prophet. We read that he returned to Galilee and encouraged those who came to hear him to cultivate a deep spiritual life. He also spoke boldly and critically of the injustice that was present in Israel-Palestine.

Fortunately, there were records kept, both in oral form and later in written form. We learn from these records that his values are expressed in his actions and his teaching, and while our records are modest, we are able to understand his mission both in the content of his teaching and his care for the sick and disenfranchised. We learn that he challenged the leadership of Israel, prophetically calling for justice and peace. He had lived with integrity in expressing these values as a healer, teacher, and prophet. He lived out the values about which he spoke, and those around him knew he was true to those values. Many people came to hear him speak and brought the sick to be healed. The religious leaders saw him as a possible threat.

THE IDENTITY OF JESUS

Jesus has been identified and described by scholars and sages in many ways over the past twenty centuries. I have been sufficiently motivated to read in detail the views of many of these accounts and have been able to sample many others. I have learned that one of best ways to learn about his identity is, quite simply, to review what he said and did, no small task in that so much has been written about him. My view is that he was a great teacher, a compassionate healer, and a courageous prophet, affirming no sectarian and cultic religious life, but one based on truth, love, justice, and peace.

There are the traditional Christian titles that reflect his identity, understanding him as prophet, priest, and king. There are also the shortened titles that are present in the New Testament, in which he is called Lord and Savior. Christians have affirmed his calling as prophet and priest and have also elevated his identity to being part of the Trinity: Father, Son, and Holy Spirit. Those outside of the Christian tradition may find some of these theological views a bit hard to accept, especially the view that he was divine. How could a first-century rabbi/teacher be divine? We in the Christian faith even ask, "How could a first-century teacher from an isolated corner of Israel-Palestine be given such grand titles?"

In the last two centuries, there has been a major focus on understanding the Jesus of history with some reluctance to describe him as divine. I want to speak more about the Jesus of history as our model, fully aware that there are a number of issues that are not fully settled in this quest to understand Jesus in his historical context. Yet it is possible, knowing that the research about his identity will not likely ever be fully completed, to lift from this extraordinary quest for the historical Jesus the three categories mentioned earlier to describe his identity: healer, teacher, and prophet. These three categories, I believe, will point us toward understanding how to embrace "the heart and mind of Jesus" as a way to live in a demanding and perilous world.

First, we note as we read the Gospels that an integral part of the identity and mission of Jesus was to heal the sickness of individuals and empower them to return to their normal life. Again and again, as we read the Gospels, we see Jesus in the presence of those who are sick and have limited resources to assist them in being healed. There are those who were blind, those who were paralytic, those who were hungry to the point of starving, and those who were mistreated and abused by those in power. An integral part of the ministry of Jesus was to heal and help this vast population.

Matthew records the story of the man with a withered hand who had gone to a synagogue to be encouraged and get help. It was a sabbath day, and he thought he might get some help from his religious friends who were attending a service. As Jesus approached him, he met some Pharisees who had heard about Jesus and his healing power. The question that was asked was whether it was lawful to cure a sick person on the Sabbath. Was healing "work" that should not be undertaken on the Sabbath? Jesus replied to the question with another question, whether one of them would remove a sheep that had fallen into a pit on the Sabbath. He said, "'Suppose one of you has only one sheep, and it falls into a pit on the Sabbath; will you not lay hold of it and lift it out? How much more valuable is a human being than a sheep! So, it is lawful to do good on the Sabbath.' Then he said to the man, 'Stretch out your hand.' He stretched it out, and it was restored, as sound as the other. But the Pharisees went out and conspired against him, how to destroy him" (Matt 12:9–14). In this incident, we learn that:

1. Healing those who were sick and had disabilities was a very high priority in the life and mission of Jesus.
2. Healing was so important that it could be done on a Sabbath day.
3. Jesus cared deeply about those who were ill and had disabilities and gave their healing a high priority.
4. It was permitted to heal on the Sabbath; healing should not be described as work that can't be done on the Sabbath.

One major feature of the identity of Jesus was to heal and care for those who suffer. It was a higher priority than to abide by a misguided interpretation of not working on the Sabbath. It is acceptable to do good on the Sabbath day.

Note as well that an integral part of the ministry of Jesus was to teach people how to live wisely and well. He is known, almost more than by any other part of his mission, as a great teacher. Part of his great abilities as a teacher was the way that he taught people about life, about values, and about how to live in a meaningful and gratifying way. One day when was teaching some of the values of the Sermon on the Mount, he slightly shifted the emphasis and focused on the priority and importance of love: "But I say unto you that listen, Love your enemies, do good to those who hate you, bless those who curse you, pray for those who abuse you. If anyone strikes you on the cheek, offer the other also; and from anyone who takes away your coat do not withhold even your shirt. Give to everyone who begs from you; and if anyone takes away your goods, do not ask for them again. Do to others as you would have them do to you" (Luke 6:27–31).

Jesus, the great teacher, goes to the heart of the matter (unconditional love) in reference to personal ethics:

1. Love is the highest priority in our lives, even if we are busy and in stressful situations. We even are especially asked to love as the one who as being cursed and abused by another person.
2. Even if another person strikes you, do not let anger overtake you, but "turn the other cheek."
3. And there will be those whose need is so great that they may steal from you. Don't ask for what is stolen back, but "do to others as you would have them do to you."

Jesus, the great teacher, says that unconditional love is the most important value in life.

Jesus was also a great prophet, one who was able to see in personal conversations shades of prejudice and discrimination. He saw that a shade of discrimination was even present in the laws and customs of the country. Jesus had the courage to speak prophetically, pointing out the presence of injustice in the social order. At one point, he spoke about the judgment that may come to countries who have abused minorities and have laws that are unjust. Matthew cites the saying of Jesus about injustice in the following way:

> When the Son of Man comes in his glory, and all the angels with him, he will sit on the throne of his glory. All the nations will be gathered before him, and he will separate people one from another as a shepherd separates the sheep from the goats, and he will put the sheep at his right hand and the goats at the left. Then the king will say to those at his right hand, "Come, you are blessed by my Father, inherit the kingdom prepared for you from the foundation of the world; for I was hungry and you gave me food, I was thirsty and you gave me something to eat, I was a stranger and you welcomed me, I was naked and you gave me clothing, I was sick and you took care of me, I was in prison and you visited me." Then the righteous will answer him, "Lord, when was it that we saw you hungry and gave you food, or thirsty and gave you something to drink? And when was it when we saw you as a stranger and welcomed you, or naked and gave you clothing? And when was it when we saw you sick or in prison and visited you?" And the king will answer them, "Truly I tell you just as you did it to one of the least of these who are members of my family, you did it to me." (Math 25:31–40)

The writer of the Gospel, sounding as though he has heard Jesus speak on many occasions and watched him care for and love people, stresses that

Jesus is a prophet who condemns injustice! And he calls for justice so that all may be safe and have the necessities of life. We hear him say, "Truly I tell you, just as you did not do it to one of the least of these, you did not do it to me" (Matt 25:45–46).

1. God blesses those who help people in need.
2. God will honor those who seek justice in the social structures.
3. Peace will come to the society that cares for its citizens and is just in its social structures and laws.
4. It is in a just society that there will be ways for individuals and governments to be at peace with one another.

Jesus the prophet says that a just society brings blessings and peace for all the people.

QUESTIONS FOR REFLECTION AND DISCUSSION

1. In what ways are you currently helping others?
2. Do you desire to be more engaged in helping others?
3. Do you feel able and sufficiently gifted to truly help others?
4. In what ways are you able to balance the concern for your own well-being with your desire to help others?
5. What are your special gifts and abilities for helping others, and what are some ways you feel inadequate to help others?

BOOKS TO CONSULT

1. Karen Armstrong, *Twelve Steps to a Compassionate Life*
2. Steven G. Post, *Unlimited Love: Altruism, Compassion, and Service*
3. David Richo, *How to Be an Adult in Relationships: The Five Keys to Mindful Loving*
4. Frank Rogers Jr., *The Way of Jesus: Compassion in Practice*
5. William C. Spohn, *Go and Do Likewise: Jesus and Ethics*

Chapter Nine

The Spirit of God in the Body of Christ

Live by the Spirit, I say, and do not gratify the desires of the flesh. For what the flesh desires is opposed to the Spirit, and what the Spirit desires is opposed to the flesh; for these desires are opposed to each other, to prevent you from doing what you want. But if you are led by the Spirit, you are not subject to the law. Now the works of the flesh are obvious: fornication, impurity, licentiousness, idolatry, sorcery, enmities, strife, jealousy, anger, quarrels, dissensions, factions, envy, drunkenness, carousing, and things like these. . . .

By contrast, the fruit of the Spirit is love, joy, peace, patience, kindness, generosity, faithfulness, gentleness, and self-control. There is no law against such things.

—Galatians 5:16–23

INTRODUCTION

We are engaged in the task of exploring how we might have a good measure of the heart and mind of Jesus within us. Living as we do in a demanding and perilous world, we need both the heart and mind of Jesus, as they are available to us, to cope with life's stresses and to thrive in our challenging setting and world. We believe that we can learn from his life and teaching how to flourish even though we know we live in difficult times and the threat to us and the well-being of the human family are real. It is no longer a homiletical gimmick to say we are in deep trouble, just as a way to get the attention of an audience. The statement that we are threatened by a wide range of natural and social dangers is an accurate description of what exists.

There were severe problems in the first century as well, ones that Jesus encountered and about which he spoke. He sensed that he had been asked by God to help those who suffered and needed guidance on how to live in such a perilous environment. He gave himself to helping people find a good and true life, healing, teaching, and addressing the social problems that kept many in poverty and as victims of injustice. He also asked others to join with him in the mission to help make life better for those who suffer and need healing and a new direction for their life.

The Christian church was formed, following the death of Jesus, to sustain his message and continue his work. There was the deep belief that how he lived, what he said, and how he died yet remained with his followers was worth sharing. This new message had the capacity to transform, heal, and give us meaning and purpose in life. Those renewed by this message became the church, and new communities based on the Jesus event formed. The new converts, called Christians, began learning how to live wisely in the difficult circumstances of their changing world.

The story of Jesus and his teaching initially spread within the Jewish community in Israel-Palestine and beyond, although there were leaders in the Jewish community who did not fully accept this new development. A young Pharisee, Saul (who later became known as Paul), strongly resisted the movement and began to persecute the new converts to what became Christianity.

While in Damascus persecuting new Christians, Saul had an unusual and profound experience, hearing a voice saying, "'Saul, Saul, why do you persecute me?' Saul replied, 'Who are you, Lord?' The reply came, 'I am Jesus, whom you are persecuting. But get up and enter the city, and you will be told what you are to do'" (Acts 9:4–6). Paul was converted, and after an extended period of reflection, he became a missionary in the young Christian movement. Following visits to several regions of the Roman Empire where had founded new churches, he wrote letters to these new churches, guiding them on the mission and message of their new faith.

THE GOOD NEWS OF LIFE IN THE SPIRIT AND THE GROWTH OF THE CHURCH

Paul traveled extensively across the Roman Empire to spread the message of Jesus. It was not easy work. His life was threatened, and, on occasion, he was imprisoned; it was a dangerous undertaking.[1] Yet he never wavered in his commitment to share the good news of Jesus. We can only sample what he taught and accomplished, and I want to focus on his teaching about how faith in Jesus was transformative for the believer. We turn to the passages in the letters to the new church in Rome and to the Galatian church(es), about how the Spirit of God is able to use the message of Jesus to transform new Christians, giving them the heart and mind of Jesus in a demanding and perilous world.

Paul's starting point, as he began his missionary work, often in Jewish settings, was to speak about the fundamental shift in the way in which we understand how God is relating to and communicating with the human family. He asserts that in the Jewish faith, which was his heritage, God engaged the human family by providing a divine law, which believers should follow. It is present in the Hebrew Scriptures, with Torah (the first five books) as foundational and then supplemented by other writings of the prophets that address ethics and the spiritual life. The shorthand version of the guiding Scripture is often referred to as "the law and prophets."

Paul, rooted and grounded in this tradition, continues to value it, but affirms that God has now spoken to humankind with an emphasis on the saving power of Jesus and the guidance of the Holy Spirit. The new convert, Paul, now asserts that the value of the law is to help us understand our need; we do not live up to the standards of the law (Rom 7:7–12). He is quite personal as he speaks about the law. He is now aware that he cannot always live up to the range of commands in the law, and, therefore, is profoundly grateful for God's grace and forgiveness. Jesus came, and now through his extraordinary life and death, we can be forgiven and empowered by God's Spirit. The new way of being in relationship with God is primarily relational rather than transactional. He writes, "There is therefore now no condemnation for those who are in Christ Jesus. For the law of the Spirit in Christ Jesus has set you free from the law of sin and death" (Rom 8:1–2).

1. There are a large number of excellent books on the life and work of Paul. See Borg and Crossan, *First Paul* and the extensive study of Paul in the two-volume work by N. T. Wright, *Paul and the Faithfulness of God.*

Paul expands his description of the new life available to those who have been transformed by the Spirit of God and contrasts it with those who are still driven by their own needs. He speaks of these two ways of living, one in the Spirit and one in the flesh. To live in the flesh is to gratify the negative impulses that are present within us and are harmful to us and to others. Paul uses the phrase to describe one living by flesh as being self-centered and driven by harmful impulses. Paul lists this behavior, calling it "the works of the flesh": "fornication, impurity, licentiousness, idolatry, sorcery, enmities, strife, jealousy, anger, quarrels, dissensions, factions, envy, drunkenness, carousing, and things like these" (Gal 5:19–21).

As I read this list, I do sometimes think that Paul may have been just a bit uptight, but on second glance, I see how these behaviors occur when one is profoundly self-centered and is controlled by impulses that are harmful. There is a kind of sickness present, one that desperately needs healing. These behaviors not only hurt the one who is driven by them, but they hurt others as well. Each one in its own way has the power to be harmful to those present when they are expressed, and as they are repeated, they have the power to become addictive. If fact, as the apostle Paul lists them, he implies that they may become a way of life that is a form of emotional sickness that needs healing. These behaviors are dangerous as they have the capacity to hurt everyone who is present when they are expressed. Paul affirms that the expression of this behavior is a sign of one who is sick and needs help.

Paul also lists the behavior of one who is mature, one who has the presence of God within them, one who is motivated by the Spirit of God. He writes, "By contrast, the fruit of the Spirit is love, joy, peace, patience, kindness, generosity, faithfulness, gentleness, and self-control" (Gal 5:22–23). He affirms there is no law against such behavior. In fact, we need to cultivate these virtues by being open to the Spirit's presence in our lives.

THE SPIRIT-FILLED LIFE

The well-educated Paul, as he writes to the Galatian church, draws upon his study of the Hebrew Bible and the Judaism that he practiced, to add nuance to what it means to be filled with the Spirit. He speaks about a deep transformation that takes place, not just a slight shift of a few religious practices.[2] There is in his writing a synthesis of Israelite literature, Jewish literature, and his own experience to say, "By contrast, the fruit of the Spirit

2. See Levison, *Filled with the Spirit*.

is love, joy, peace, patience, kindness, generosity, faithfulness, gentleness, and self-control. There is no law against such things. And those who belong to Christ Jesus have crucified the flesh with its passions and desires. If we live by the Spirit, let us also be guided by the Spirit" (Gal 5:22–25).

This new way of life was a contrast to the one that was characteristic of many of his readers, those driven by inner turmoil and in conflict with those in their immediate circle of relationships. Paul implies in this letter that the dominant culture was filled with conflict and competition, and he wants to be sure that the new church does not have a culture where there is unhealthy competition between people and envy in reference to those in power. Paul understands that the behavior in the Galatian church will influence the attitude and spirit within an environment and culture that is deeply rooted in sexual abuse, conflict, competing points of view, and harmful behavior. It was not a setting where one might encounter a spiritual way of life and an ethical outlook rooted in sustaining a humane and just way of life.

We are fortunate to have the results of excellent research in psychology and sociology that will help us understand the problems faced by the new church(es) in Galatia. I want to suggest some ways for us to avoid behavior that threatens and hurts others and to engage to create a church setting that contributes to healthy spiritual formation and responsible behavior.

Over the years, I have reflected on how it is that those of us at the ground level and with limited resources may still contribute to creating a healthy congregation rather than being passive and just becoming part of the problem. The first step has been to engage in a better understanding the problem. I have tried to discern its causes, and, with others, have sought to identify the current situation. It is not enough to just agree that there is problem; we have to understand the nature of the problem, how it is having a negative impact on groups of people, what solutions have been tried, and how we might help in creating a new church environment. The first step is to understand, to *see* all of the different dimensions of the problem.

Next, as we were able to see the many dimensions of the problem, we began to wonder what we might do to help. We moved to the second word, be, in the *see-be-do* formula. Did we have the experience and talent that might be helpful in finding a good solution? What skills would we need if we wanted to help? How might we gain more information in order offer some assistance? And how might we adjust our outlook about the problem in order to be helpful rather than just to complain or accuse others of making the problem worse? First, we needed to *see*, then we needed to *be*, that is to become a group that can make a contribution to improving the situation.

The third step, following the need to see clearly and then become a group that might help, was to search carefully for good solutions. We didn't need to be those with just a negative presence, often a great risk. We moved on to the *do* stage, one that logically followed the *see* and *be* stages.

In short, I needed to move toward finding good solutions to problems. We needed to see, to be, and to do; see clearly, be a person who could help in an active way, and then understand what we could do to help. We needed to be a see-be-do group, and I confess that it was easy to stop at the *see* stage, difficult to move to the *be* stage, and very difficult to move to the *do* stage.

GUIDANCE

We are endeavoring in this writing to understand how we might cultivate the same mind and spirit as Jesus as we seek to do our part in creating a more just and humane world. How might we be better prepared to help make a contribution in our part of the world that will encourage the formation of a setting in which truth is sought and honored, love and compassion are present, and justice prevails so that no one is discriminated against or left out of the opportunities. We have used the church as the setting in which to make our contribution, a setting where peace prevails and people are able to make good choices.

First, we need to *see clearly*, as our Jain brothers and sisters teach in their formula for maturity: right seeing, right knowledge, and right conduct. Right seeing is to understand the setting in which we live, right knowledge is to understand the nature of change in order to contribute to making our setting safe and just, and right conduct is being involved in making the necessary changes.

We start with being educated in order to see. What are the truths and conditions that we need to understand? We know that only truth can support the great weight of the future. So, we start by looking at the process of change, what has been called "The Five Stages of Permanent Change."[3] They are:

3. I regret not having a reference for this list of stages for permanent change. Once again, I likely received it in a workshop or heard it in a lecture at some point in my career, put it in a file, and now am able to use it. I give full credit to the one who prepared the

1. Pre-contemplation (before careful thought) stage: a period of time when we don't fully know all the problems that need our attention, but sense that they exist and are asking for attention
2. Contemplation stage: when we acknowledge there is a specific problem and we begin to think about a solution
3. Preparation stage: when we begin to plan for action, but still feel some ambivalence and need vision and encouragement, perhaps even approval
4. Action stage: when we begin to modify our behavior, change our surroundings, and get permission to engage in change
5. Maintenance stage: when we make a firm commitment to make the changes, having permission and assembling the team to make the change, and then do it

And I would add another stage:

6. Completion stage: when we have made the changes, perhaps feel some nostalgia or even regret, but have the courage to stay with the changes and assess their value

PREPARATION AND PROCESS

It is vitally important that we prepare ourselves as we seek to have the mind and spirit of Jesus as we face the hard realities of living in a demanding and perilous world. I have reflected often on what it means to be a spiritual person who is empowered to live wisely and well. As I have read the various definitions of being a spiritual person, I have learned that to be spiritual is to open one's heart to the full presence of God. Indeed, as we have maintained, it is to have the heart and mind of Jesus. It was Jesus who spoke about the reign of God in one's life, and it is Jesus who is the model of one who opened his life fully to the reign of God. It involved the sensitive feelings of his heart, the understanding of his mind, and the commitment of his will to be ready to respond to the tug of God. It means having one's emotional life in tune with God, feeling close to God, able to sense the will and way of God and have the capacity to respond in loving and thoughtful obedience. It is to prepare our spirit, our deep center, and then to sense the

list, although I have changed it some.

guiding hand of God. To be truly spiritual is to place our faith in God and then to make the commitment to the will and way of God. In the Christian faith, there is the emphasis on understanding the will and way of God expressed and modeled in the life and teaching of Jesus. We seek to follow Jesus and to pattern our lives on the values he lived and taught.

THE PLACE OF THE HEALTHY COMMUNITY

For one to have the heart and mind of Jesus in a demanding and perilous world, there will be the need for the support, the encouragement, and the counsel of others. As I say that a community is essential, I am reminded that many of the great spiritual leaders, within the Christian tradition and also in other faith communities, have sought the deep spiritual life in isolation, away from all of the distracting influences of modern life. I honor these endeavors, and I have found that being alone and quiet, stopping a while from the mad race of contemporary life, was a way to gain inner peace and perspective on the swirl around us. Yet, even as I have used the personal retreat as a way to center my life, I know that I need others to guide my meditation and the learning and the resources of a community for emotional support. I know that I belong, even as I am alone in prayer. I need a circle of trust.

The word "formation" has been frequently used to describe spiritual growth and development, although words change as fast as generations come and go. I learn from the Sacred Art of Living Center for Spiritual Formation[4] that formation assumes that there is a "home base" of truth, although described in a variety of ways across the centuries. Words such as soul, spirit, and heart are often used, and for these dimensions of my identity, I need a center or quiet space for the truth to be present. The mind is also a factor, helpful in most cases, but occasionally distracting. It is in that center that I open my heart to the fullness of God, the Spirit, or the truth. As I remain still and focused, I reclaim my wholeness and identity, and understand with increasing clarity the relationship between my meditation and my calling to service in the world.

I am able to experience this wholeness and call, in some measure, because I am part of a community, the church, in which I have found a home

4. I am grateful for the guidance of a 2006 publication of the Sacred Art of Living Center for Spiritual Formation, material I obtained from the Center for Courage and Renewal.

that has the following qualities that are foundational, although occasionally absent. My Ten Commandments in this community are:

- I have been truly welcomed, not because "this is what we do" but because I am worthy of being present and receiving hospitality. I am valued.
- I am truly present, able in a variety of ways to be there for others even with some doubt and fear as well as some gifts and love to share.
- I am received by sincere invitation, not there to checked off as present, but to offer my gifts and abilities.
- While present, I am able to speak the truth while accepting the way others understand truth, and together, we enrich one another. There is integrity in what we believe and what we say.
- I am not there not to make changes, to fix what is broken, or to set other people straight about how to live, but let who I am be my contribution.
- While there, I am able to respond to others, to have integrity with my questions, and to help in listening to others in a way that empowers them to be honest.
- When there is tension, perhaps deep differences and fear about being accepted, I accept others without judgment, listen to them, and learn.
- I pay attention to my own "inner teacher," that part of me that may be able to make a contribution to others, and so I pay attention to my feelings, sensing the responses of others, and participate in ongoing life of the community.
- Be sure to trust the value of silence, get some relief from the noisy world, be a part of the group by listening and affirming, and avoid filling each moment of quiet with words.
- It is there that I am able to hear the voice of God, yet only when I stop judging and am quiet, when I truly love the others who are present, and I silently tune in to the Loving Presence.

QUESTIONS FOR REFLECTION AND DISCUSSION

1. In what sort of context did the early church form and become a community?

2. What was Paul's perspective on the new church, and how did it change?
3. How do you understand the term "life in the Spirit," and how might such an outlook change your way of life?
4. What does Paul mean when he talks about "life in the flesh"?
5. What sort of community or support do you need in order to live as you want to live?

BOOKS TO CONSULT

1. John R. Levison, *Filled with the Spirit*
2. Thomas Merton, *Contemplation in a World of Action*
3. Stephen G. Post, *Unlimited Love: Altruism, Compassion, and Service*
4. Frank Rogers Jr., *Compassion in Practice*
5. Roger Walsh, *Essential Spirituality: The 7 Central Practices to Awaken Heart and Mind*

Chapter Ten

The Mind and Heart of Jesus with Us to the End

It was now about noon, and darkness came over the whole land until three in the afternoon, while the sun's light failed; and the curtain of the temple was torn in two. Then, Jesus, crying with a loud voice, said, "Father, into your hands I commend my spirit."

—Luke 23:46

INTRODUCTION

Much has been written about the end of the life of Jesus. I have read several of these accounts and have been helped and nurtured by many of them. They give the reader a frame of reference for understanding a central component of the Christian faith. We hear in our churches that "Jesus died for our sins," and this short sentence became an integral part of the church's understanding of redemption. The death of Jesus paid the price to set us free from the slavery of sin, and we are now by faith set free to become one with God, cultivate and deepen our faith, live the spiritual life, and engage in service.

As we read the biblical accounts carefully, we discover that there is the concurrent meaning of the death of Jesus; we are given the model of Jesus, one who teaches us how to live our faith and cope with the end of life. As we read the story of the last few days of his life, we are enriched and deeply moved. As we read, we are guided on how best to face the end of our life.

The context in which Jesus was crucified had a particular character. Prior to that final day, Jesus had come to Jerusalem with his disciples to complete what he believed was his mission in life. He had taught, healed, and proclaimed his message in the Galilee and in the adjacent areas of Israel-Palestine. He ministered in these ways for an extended period of time, perhaps for nearly three years.[1] There was the occasional trip south to Jerusalem, but his focus in the public ministry was in the region from which he had come. His ministry included healing, teaching his message of love, and challenging some of the traditional teaching of the religious leaders, primarily the Pharisees, in reference to the way the law was interpreted. The issue of what is meant by "work" in reference to the Sabbath came up, as Jesus healed and helped people on the Sabbath. As he became known, large groups of people came to hear him and on several occasions asked for help with healing and for guidance in reference to their religious beliefs and practices.

Healing was a very central part of his ministry. For example, the Gospel writers speak of his ability to heal those with leprosy.[2] Luke writes, "Once, when he was in one of the cities, there was a man covered with leprosy. When he saw Jesus, he bowed with his face to the ground and begged him, 'Lord, if you choose you can make me clean.' Then Jesus stretched out his hand, touched him, and said, 'I do choose. Be made clean.' Immediately the leprosy left him. Jesus then ordered him to tell no one. 'Go,' he said, 'and show yourself to the priest, and, as Moses commanded, make an offering for your cleansing, for a testimony to them.' But now more than ever the word about Jesus spread abroad; many crowds would gather to hear him and to be cured of their diseases" (Luke 5:12–15).

Conversations with the religious leaders covered several subjects, one of which was the interpretation of the Sabbath observance. On one occasion, Jesus was walking with his disciples on the Sabbath, and his disciples plucked the heads of grain, rubbed them in their hands, and ate the nourishing part. They were hungry. The Pharisees questioned Jesus about this occurrence, suggesting it involved work on the Sabbath. Jesus replied that even David, the great king, did something akin to what his disciples had done, implying that preparing food and eating on the Sabbath was

1. There continues to be some scholarly debate about the length of the public ministry of Jesus. The traditional three years continues to be believed by many, although there are reputable scholars who maintain that this period of the life of Jesus was shorter.

2. The lepers who came to him may have had what modern medicine calls leprosy, but in the time of Jesus, it may have referred to some other diseases as well.

legitimate (Luke 6:1–5). Jesus was teaching that rest on the Sabbath was to foster good health, and that picking grain to eat was not work to be avoided, but just a matter of having food to eat in order to stay healthy.

As one reviews incidents such as those above and many others reported in the Gospel records, we see clearly that Jesus was engaged in practices that invited some questioning by the religious leaders, although the practices were legitimate. In fact, they were a great blessing as reported in the two incidents referred to above. These incidents not only spoke to those present with him, but also to us; we too are called to love others and help them improve their lives.

THE LESSONS OF LIFE

We find in the Gospels the consistent message to love God with one's whole being and to love others as we love ourselves; it is the central ethical message of Jesus. As we read about his life, his ministry to all who came to him, and his final days, we learn about caring for those in need and long to have the heart and mind of Jesus who loved others and gave himself to the will and way of God.

One lesson we learn, often right from the start, is that to have the heart and mind of Jesus in our daily lives *will be difficult*. To love others will not always be easy. In fact, it can be quite difficult when many of those in the category of "others" are not all that lovable.

It is also important to note that love is not always just a feeling of attraction or admiration. Occasionally, those close to us can be very easy to love; we like who they are and their presence in our lives is positive and contributes to our well-being. Yet the teaching and model of Jesus is to love those who may be ill, may be emotionally stressed, may have values different from our ours, and may come from a very different culture with practices that seem strange to us. The love that Jesus models is *inclusive*, and it is not just about positive feelings. Very often it is about practice, helping others who may be difficult to help. We accept and receive others who are different from us and offer a loving response, even if the circumstances require us to lend a hand and help those who are very difficult to love. In short, we love them even if they do not meet our required standard of attractiveness, goodness, and other common values. Jesus loved the leper, the woman at the well, and the one who collected taxes.

The second lesson I learn is that we must continue *to trust God and that we will be empowered by the Spirit of God to love* those who are needy and may not be attractive to us. God gives what God asks. I find in many situations where I am with others different from me and who are not all that lovable that I do need the empowering presence of God within me to truly love them. I need to be open to the Spirit of God to help me to have the heart and mind of Jesus as I meet those who need a loving response or action, even if there are not always warm feelings of attraction.

A third lesson I have learned over the years is *humility*. There will be times when I am the needy one, not the gifted and attractive leader who carries all the responsibilities for including strangers and helping others. I have had to learn this lesson often across the years of my daily life and in my service. I am not always able to love others, and I have learned to turn to God to be empowered to love. In humility, I have learned that God gives what God expects and requires. I am not always consistent in my attempt to be a loving person, yet in faith, God helps me to be the one who brings loving care to those who are left out of the circle of love.

Part of my inability to be able to make friends and help them immediately as I first meet them stems from my childhood and background, one in which I did not always feel worthy or attractive. My poor self-image occasionally caused me to withdraw from settings where love was needed. My low regard for myself is partially rooted in the way my father treated me in my childhood. He wanted me to *excel in everything*, which I was unable to do. He would remind me, when what I had done was less than perfect, that I must work harder in order to excel in my school work and my participation in sports. When I got his message, with little praise, I found that I needed to be alone.

I would often retreat and find something I could do when I was alone and wouldn't be judged. For example, I became a consistent reader, knowing that I would not be rejected. The family environment has left me being somewhat reluctant to take the first steps toward friendship. The result has been that I have occasionally felt left out, although it was likely more my withdrawal as an introvert than the actions of others. In short, even in the adult years, there have been times when I do not feel acceptable or able to meet the expectations of others. I know now that I will likely be accepted when I reach out to anther for conversation and friendship, yet there is still the whisper of not being acceptable or attractive. There are still traces of the insecurity because my father always wanted me to excel so *he could feel proud around others.*

In addition, I still feel some insecurity because the circumstances of my family were unsettled. My father's jobs changed several times following World War II, and I had to attend four different elementary schools. I did not have time to feel like I belonged. I often felt alone and not included. I didn't have the time to develop long-term friendships, and I fell behind in my school work. It wasn't until middle school that I had more than a year in one setting and had time to cultivate deep friendships.

I also found that each school I attended had a different approach to education. It wasn't until the sixth grade that I began to feel like I actually understood that each year was built on the progress of the previous year, that education was cumulative. Yet even then, I still had the tendency to want to demonstrate in some tangible way that I was really okay. I worked hard to get good grades, partially to prove I was acceptable. I felt a need for others to know I had some talent. It wasn't until late in high school that I began to be more comfortable with just being who I am. Yet the traces of the feeling of not being acceptable have followed me into adulthood.

Moving into a faith orientation in late high school helped some in that I was assured that I was acceptable in reference to God's love, and that I could be loved by others and learn how to love others. I also got acquainted with those who had comparable feelings of not being acceptable, a not uncommon characteristic of the middle school years. I gradually began to accept that I could be liked for who I am, although the feelings of not being smart enough or attractive enough have continued in some measure through my adult years. Those who know me have reassured me in several ways that I am acceptable, but the little ugly and dumb boy comes along in my backpack.

THE SENIOR YEARS

I am now in my senior years and wanting to be at peace, to relax, and to just be. I am hopeful that my lifetime of experiences and my growth as a person will help me to live with gratitude for who I am and what I have done. I do find a measure peace within, and my well-informed faith has helped me see more clearly the contours of the peaceful life.

I am trying to learn directly from the life of Jesus how to manage these years. Although we don't have sufficient information to trace the early years of the life of Jesus, it appears that he did have a measure of security and love in his early years. From all we know, Mary and Joseph were loving parents, and he likely had siblings at home with which to share the experiences of growing up and becoming a responsible adult.

We do learn that because of his deep conviction to serve God, he left his practice as a craftsman, visited his cousin John the Baptist, went on a retreat in the wilderness near the Dead Sea, and then became a teacher and prophet. He moved into a very public life, initially serving his home region of the Galilee with many side trips to adjacent regions. He was loved by those whom he served, helped, and healed, but began to face opposition from the religious and political leaders. His message and healing were questioned by those in power. The end of his life came prematurely because he did bring truth to power, as did the Hebrew prophets before him. He was arrested for challenging those in power and teaching and preaching the values of truth, love, peace, and justice. His life and teaching have provided wisdom and ethical guidance across the centuries, and what he modeled and taught is applicable to nearly all the stages of life.

We do have a record of his final days. After his arrest, he continued to speak the truth and affirm that love is the guiding ethical norm for all people and that justice makes peace possible. He had reached the age of full maturity, even in his early thirties. Fortunately, we do have an account of "the heart and mind of Jesus" at the end of his life. It is one of the most inspiring and insightful accounts of how to live at the end of life. It is a true treasure for all.

JESUS AT THE END OF LIFE

"From that time on, Jesus began to show his disciples that he must go to Jerusalem and undergo great suffering at the hands of the elders and the chief priests and scribes, and be killed and on the third day to be raised" (Matt 16:21). The opposition to Jesus had become quite intense and direct. There was within Jesus that sense that his life work had not been completed, and that he had to go to Jerusalem to complete his mission in life.

Jesus and his immediate followers do stop on the way to Jerusalem, find a place to camp in a region with modest mountains, and have serious conversations about what might happen in Jerusalem. Jesus seems to know there will be opposition to his teaching and healing, perhaps by the Romans and more likely in the Sanhedrin, the regional governmental body of the Jews. His disciples have some questions about whether it is wise to go to where there is so much opposition, but Jesus says that they must go. Then the group has an extraordinary experience, called the transfiguration. They sense that they are in the presence of the great leaders of the Jewish people, Moses and Elijah, and now understand that they must continue to follow their plan to go to Jerusalem (Matt 17:1–13).

As they continue to Jerusalem, there are some conversations in which Jesus explains to his small group, known later as his apostles, why they must go. Matthew describes several encounters with people as they travel on to Jerusalem. There is the conversation with the rich young man, one who does not commit to following Jesus because he wants to keep his wealth, knowing that to follow Jesus would mean to use the wealth to help those in need. There are some little children who come to him, and he blesses them. As they walk, Jesus continues his ministry of teaching about life concerns such as forgiveness and divorce, and he continues the practice of teaching in parables with the story of lost sheep, underlining that their ministry is to "the lost sheep." The chronology of the time following the transfiguration is not altogether clear, but their destination is clear.[3] They arrive in the outskirts of Jerusalem, find places to stay, and prepare themselves for the coming week.

In another part of greater Jerusalem, other conversations are occurring. It is the time of Passover, and the city is crowded, almost double in size for this special week of religious observance. Religious leaders are present for these holidays, and there are hundreds of people who fill the streets, seeking housing or campsites and hoping to find food. Jesus and the disciples have found places to stay and meet to discuss the week and celebrate the feast of Passover, a very important holiday in Jewish life.

As they gather for this meal, now called the Lord's Supper, one of them sneaks away to betray Jesus. There is the recognition by Jesus that Judas may betray them, although Judas denies that he will do it. As Jesus guides his disciples during the meal, there is conversation about one at the table who may betray him, and Peter says that he would never betray Jesus. As the meal concludes, they sing a hymn and go to the Mount of Olives. Jesus goes to the garden of Gethsemane to pray; it is the middle of the night, and those with him sleep. Jesus does not sleep but "wrestles" with God, praying, "My Father, if it be possible, let this cup pass from me; yet not what I want, but what you want" (Matt 26:39).

3. Matthew's Gospel includes a range of teachings and conversations on the way, although the chronology is not precise.

Very early in the morning, after the night of prayer, Jesus is aware that soldiers are coming to arrest him. Peter resists the soldiers, there is an exchange, Jesus is arrested, and the disciples leave him. Jesus is taken to the high priest, and there is another brief conversation about whether Jesus is the long-expected Messiah. There are also some questions about which authority should try Jesus, the Sanhedrin or perhaps the ruler in Galilee where Jesus is from. The decision is made to send him to the Roman leader, in that his teaching may be considered a capital offense, one for which the guilty person may be crucified. He is sent to Pilate, the Roman person with authority in the region.

In the background, there are those watching the proceedings. For example, Peter is identified as a follower of Jesus because his accent is that of a person from Galilee. Peter denies he is one of those close to Jesus, and then remembers that he said he would never betray Jesus.

As all of this is happening, Judas, suffering from guilt for having betrayed Jesus, commits suicide. Pilate says he will free one person of the three who have come before him in the Roman court. Jesus is questioned by Pilate, and there are those in the resistance by the crowd that has assembled to observe the trial and crucifixion of Jesus. There are two others who have been arrested and come before Pilate as well. Pilate, somewhat overwhelmed by the crowd, says he will set free one of the three criminals before him and invites the crowd to help him decide which one it will be. There is some action behind the scenes, and the crowd does not select Jesus. The crowd prevails and Jesus now faces crucifixion, and the soldiers make Jesus carry his cross to the place where he will be crucified. He carries the cross of truth, of love, of justice, and of peace.

THE CRUCIFIXION AND THE LAST SAYINGS OF JESUS.

Jesus, on his cross, is still able to speak, and he has criminals on either side of him, one with whom he speaks. Remarkably, we do have some information about the last words of Jesus on the cross. He is able to manage his fears and speak with clarity and bravery through the whole process, from the last supper with the disciples to the prayerful night in Gethsemane, the betrayals by some of his colleagues, including Peter, the appearance before members of the Sanhedrin, and the formal arrest and the sentence by Pilate. He is on the cross, and even in the midst of this intense pain and suffering, he demonstrates what it means to have faith, courage, and wisdom.

We do have a record of the last sayings of Jesus on the cross.[4] As always, the thoughtful historian will ask about their reliability. It is an important question, and there is no way to prove that Jesus spoke these exact words. Yet there were those who were eyewitnesses, and the words could have been heard and then repeated in small groups, some of which would have cared deeply about his experience on the cross. I want to use them for understanding, knowing that we are relying on the custom of the time, which was to preserve important information in an oral tradition; historical records were rare and the past was remembered by sharing what was heard by those who were present and then shared with the larger community.

1. The first saying is found in the Gospel of Luke: "Father, forgive them for they know not what they are doing" (23:34). The saying comes as Jesus is put on the cross, with criminals on either side of him. There were the soldiers who put him on the cross, and others who arranged the custom of casting lots for the clothing of the criminals. People watched and heard him speak, and they began to cast lots to divide his clothing. Those in charge had little empathy and said, "If he is the Messiah of God, he can save himself," and mocked him. The sign overhead on the cross said, "This is the king of the Jews." I am taken by the way Jesus actually cares about those who may have been forced to participate in this crucifixion. He has deep empathy for those who were commanded to do this work, soldiers who mock him, and those who cast lots for his clothing. There is forgiveness in the heart of Jesus, and we learn, as we so often do, that Jesus was able to care for those who are causing his suffering. There is forgiveness for their lack of understanding and for what the system has forced them to do. It is a demonstration of the way God forgives us.
2. The second saying is also recorded in Luke's account: "Then he said, 'Jesus, remember me when you come into your kingdom.' Jesus replied, 'Truly I tell you, today you will be with me in Paradise'" (23:43). Next to Jesus is a person who is suffering beyond measure, one who is asking Jesus, from deep inside of himself, to save his life. He is not through living, has hopes for his future, and maybe even still wants to be with and help his family. Jesus, again with profound empathy, reassures him that he will somehow, some way, continue to have

4. There are those that would say that it is difficult to affirm that Jesus actually spoke these last few words. There may be some questions about wording, but it is clear that what he is quoted as saying matches his courage and integrity.

consciousness and be with Jesus in paradise, understood as the location or status of uninterrupted bliss. There were images, as the word was used, that may have been associated with the garden of Eden. Jesus comforts the one next to him, as he himself suffers. He knows that this other person next to him longs for freedom from suffering. Jesus again cares for another person and does not focus on his own suffering. One wonders how he could be so selfless, and my answer is that we seek to have the mind and spirit of Jesus, to be as loving and sensitive as Jesus was at the end of his life.

3. Meanwhile, standing near the cross of Jesus were his mother and his mother's sister. John was also present with this small group. "When Jesus saw his mother and the disciple whom he loved standing beside her, he said to his mother, 'Woman, here is your son.' Then he said to the disciple, 'Here is your mother.'" (John 19:26–27). Once again, Jesus is demonstrating his capacity to care for his mother and entrusts her to the one who may have been his closest friend, John. Jesus continues to demonstrate his capacity, even in the midst of indescribable pain, to care for those whom he loves. His love seems to have no limits.

4. "And about three o'clock Jesus cried out with a loud voice, 'Eloi, Eloi, lema sabachthani?' that is, 'My God, My God, why have you forsaken me?'" (Matt 27:46). Jesus does feel the depth of loss, perhaps wondering why God would allow for him to suffer as he does. In this setting, we see the human side of Jesus, one that does feel enormous pain and loss and expresses it, and we honor him for sharing his suffering in a way that we can understand.

5. He also shows that he is vulnerable and has a human side when he calls out, "I am thirsty" (John 19:28). In some ways, this utterance of Jesus underlines how profoundly honest and self-revealing Jesus is as he suffers on the cross. He is one of us, gets thirsty, and asks for what he needs. He is a congruent person, with profound integrity, and lets those around him know of his suffering and need for water.

6. John does record in his record that Jesus is close to death, and that he says, "It is finished" (John 19:30). There comes a moment, as I have observed in my role as chaplain and being present with a person who is dying, that there is a release at the end of life, when one is able to say, "I now accept that I am dying." I have seen those who have been angry at this point, and others that have sensed some relief that the end has

come. Jesus is in that second category, accepting, as he does, that there is this moment when human life ends, and that we can be at peace. Jesus says, "It is finished," and he can close his eyes.

7. As he does, he says his final words: "Father, into your hands I commend my spirit" (Luke 23:46). Jesus, in this final moment, does rise above his suffering and with deep faith and trust lets go and moves into the full presence of God. I find these last experiences and words of Jesus very inspiring. They tell me that there is a pathway to the end, one that overcomes suffering. There is movement to the point of total trust in God and little need to just hang on and continue to suffer. One can place one's total trust in the God of love, even as one suffers.

I would not want to be among those who too easily say that suffering and death are easy to manage if you just trust the love of God. There is the great risk of trying to help others by giving them a sort of trite formula. What we have in the story is not a statement that the end of life, and the possible suffering that accompanies it, is without deep and profound physical and emotional pain. In fact, what we have is the opposite, showing that it is a time that may be the most difficult of all, especially if dying is preceded by a long period of suffering. What we have, as we look at the final days and hours of the life of Jesus, is our model of how we seek to have the mind and spirit of Jesus at the end.

QUESTIONS FOR REFLECTION AND DISCUSSION

1. How do you understand the crucifixion of Jesus? What was he accused of doing that caused him to be arrested and sentenced to death?
2. How did Jesus deal with the authorities who insisted that one should not work on the Sabbath?
3. How comfortable are you in the presence of strangers? Is it a bit difficult to strike up a conversation with them?
4. Do you find it easy to help those in need?
5. Which of the last sayings of Jesus on the cross has the most meaning for you?

BOOKS TO CONSULT

1. Katy Butler, *The Art of Dying Well: A Practical Guide to the Good End of Life*
2. John Gunther, *Death Be Not Proud*
3. Elisabeth Kübler-Ross, *On Death and Dying*
4. Bo Miller and Shoshana Berger, *A Beginner's Guide to the End: Practical Advice for Living Life and Facing Death*
5. Frank Ostaseski, *The Five Invitations: Discovering What Death Can Teach Us About Living Fully*

Chapter Eleven

Conclusion: The Transformed Mind and Heart as the Way to Flourish in a Troubled World

As God's chosen ones, holy and beloved, clothe yourselves with compassion, kindness, humility, meekness, and patience. Bear with one another and, if anyone has a complaint against another, forgive each other; just as the Lord has forgiven you, so you must forgive. Above all, clothe yourselves with love, which binds everything together in perfect harmony. And let the peace of Christ rule in your hearts, to which indeed you were called in the one body. And be thankful. Let the word of Christ dwell in you richly; teach and admonish one another in all wisdom, and with gratitude in your hearts, sing psalms, hymns, and spiritual songs to God. And whatever you do, in word or deed, do everything in the name of the Lord Jesus, giving thanks to God the Father through him.

—Colossians 3:12–17

INTRODUCTION

Our theme, drawn from the apostle Paul's letter to the Philippians, is "Let this same mind be in you that was in Christ Jesus" (2:5). Across the years, I have thought about and explored some of the qualities that are implied in "the same mind . . . that was in Christ Jesus." Initially, I am persuaded that the term "mind" means more than just intellectual understanding and includes a good heart and positive outlook guided by the Spirit of God. To have the mind that was in Christ Jesus, one must invite the full presence of the Holy Spirit into one's life; it is an act of faith, and then it becomes a way of life as we practice the presence of God. Paul says that the first step is to empty ourselves as Jesus did, giving up our self-centeredness, taking the form of a servant, and becoming obedient to God. Paul articulates this same theme in his letter to the Colossian church, using the metaphor of clothing ourselves with the following attire:

- Compassion, by which he means selfless and unconditional love
- Kindness, the human quality that the Dalai Lama called the essence of religious faith
- Humility, having an awareness of our need and openness to change
- Meekness, seeking a way of life that is gentle and endures the hardships of life
- Patience without resentment

Paul's word to the Philippians is to "work out your own salvation with fear and trembling; for it is God who is at work in you, enabling you both to will and work for his good pleasure" (Phil 2:12–13).

WORKING OUT YOUR SALVATION

As I write and read, I have a sense that I am in Philippi and a new convert on a faith journey, eager to understand the advice of Paul. I am persuaded that he means that we need insight, self-awareness, and tangible commitment for there to be genuine growth and development. Words such as "love" and "faith" are foundational but may not always be expanded in a way that inspires one to make these qualities an integral part of one's way of life. To cultivate one's faith and to fill one's life with love and compassion is a life journey of growth, a process that takes time, self-assessment, reflection, meditation, and focused attention. We start this new journey by taking several steps.

STEP ONE: CULTIVATING A SPIRITUAL PATHWAY

Step one in working out our salvation is to find and cultivate a personal and thoughtful spiritual pathway. Such a path needs to be ours, although it will have dimensions that are part of the spiritual path of others. But for you to be intentional about spiritual formation, you need a path that you have carefully and wisely chosen, one with your attitudes and practices. As you are informed sufficiently, it should be one that you have designed, perhaps with the help of others, but one in which you have a clear understanding, a level of comfort, and a good measure of motivation. The design should revolve around your needs and personal style of understanding and expressing your faith.

This conviction may be acknowledged by those who teach and guide people of faith, but more frequently than not, those who "help" may be inclined to teach a single way of spiritual growth. Yes, we do learn from others, there are dimensions to the spiritual pathways that are nearly universal, and our faith journey is shared by others. Yet we *need to make it our own* for the journey to reach our goal of mature spirituality. I look back on my experience of finding a spiritual pathway, and I am grateful to those who have taught and guided me. I have followed across the years the general patterns of spiritual growth, many biblically based. But with this information, I have put my own style of growing and learning in place, and I now have a way of "being" that has my name on it. I have "worked out" my own pathway of spiritual growth and practice.

One suggested pathway that has been helpful to me draws upon the insights of Carl G. Jung, one of the pioneers of human growth and development. His views do reflect an outlook of a previous era, but they also contain a perspective that applies to all of us, and one that can be easily updated. It is possible to incorporate many of his insights and categories as a framework for spiritual growth. What is especially helpful is that his frame of reference enables us to see spiritual formation as a positive component to health and happiness rather one limited to religious categories. Those who have used Jung's theory of psychological types have also tended to attach and integrate them with the Myers-Briggs Type Indicator.[1] First there is a list of the dimensions of the spiritual path, and they include action, reflection, service, awareness, knowledge, devotion, discipline, and spontaneity.

1. The material I am using for this section is from documents I received years ago from the Center for Applications of Psychological Type (CAPT).

Each one of these dimensions of our lives are classified by the following criteria: positive expressions, negative expressions, under developed, over developed, special vulnerabilities, and what is needed for wholeness. In addition, one's attitude and expression of faith are integrated into the Myers-Briggs indicator, suggesting the best patterns for one's growth may be discerned in the following categories: extroversion, introversion, sensing, intuition, thinking, feeling, judgment, and perception. Using this model will help us design a spiritual pathway that fits our unique personal style.

In the last few decades, there has been a steady shift of understanding spirituality in reference to the perilous times in which we live. In what ways should our spirituality assist us with managing life in a very troubled world? One response has been to follow the example of those who have devoted the early years of their lives to total retreat from the secular world, often joining with others in living in isolation with a clear and disciplined plan of spiritual formation.[2] Others have gone in almost a different direction and said that true spirituality is to engage in creating a more just society and working for world peace. True spirituality is not retreating from threats, but engaging in dealing with profound challenges of our time. And between the two extremes, there has been an increased interest in the spiritual life within the churches in our neighborhoods with the label of a denomination. What is common to these movements is that our spiritual life will help make us more responsible citizens, helping to create a more just and humane world beginning in our own neighborhood.

I have found that placing our way of growth and practice of spiritual formation within psychological categories and/or the quest for a more just world is a way to engage in spiritual formation. It has helped me to understand better my responsibility to seek growth toward maturity that will empower me to join in helping to create a more just and caring world. Yet I have also found that there are some differences between our psychological growth and our spiritual growth, although the two tend to be intertwined. I have also found that religious outlooks of the non-Western religions tend to add shades of meaning and alternative practices that inform and enrich those of us in the Judeo-Christian frame of reference. Spirituality within Buddhism, in its several manifestations, invites a spirituality that is often

2. I have been influenced by the life and teaching of Thomas Merton, who left his busy life and became a monk. He has written extensively about this decision to leave the "busy world of scrambling for wealth and power." Merton, *Contemplation* 172–80.

rooted in the disciplined life.[3] It shares this emphasis with other "schools" of spiritual formation that stress the dangers of giving in to the "way of the world" in the sense of valuing wealth and power and being insensitive to the poor and needy.

There are many ways to find spiritual guidance, and there is a great need to have spiritual values in a troubled world that seems to have lost its way. In fact, some of our greatest spiritual leaders have emerged in times of trouble, sharing an outlook and pattern of life in contrast to the values of wealth and power and the division of the human family into friends and enemies. I have learned so much from other religions than my own, and one has to be blind not to see spiritual wisdom in the teachings of Buddhism, Hinduism, and several other religions. There are many spiritual pathways, and given my heritage, I acknowledge that Jesus continues to be my teacher in these perilous times, but I have been so blessed by my exposure to other pathways, often sharing similar practices.

STEP TWO: INTEGRATING OUR RELIGIOUS BELIEFS, OUR COMMUNITY LIFE, OUR ETHICAL NORMS, AND OUR SPIRITUAL PRACTICES

I have tended to work with an integrated model of religious faith and practice, placing foundational beliefs, community life, ethical teaching, and spiritual practices into the broad category of nurturing healthy spirituality. In fact, in trying to discern a spiritual pathway, I have drawn upon a theological outlook that is foundational, living responsibly within a believing community that is nurturing, engaging in tangible ways to help create a just society, and sustaining these commitments in a private practice of spiritual formation. I wish I could report that it has always been easy and that there were always positive results. I can't say that, but I can say that I have made some progress by using this more integrated strategy.

On occasion, I have heard that being very disciplined in theological understanding is just "an intellectual trip" and doesn't contribute to one's spiritual formation. Yet I have found this work (yes, work) has given me a basis for my faith and my quest to pursue a spiritual life. The discipline it requires has focused on being as truthful as possible in articulating my beliefs. If finding truth is not important, then what is? On a more positive

3. See, for example, Kornfield, *Wise Heart*.

note, I have been encouraged by those who think in terms of the life-giving community, one that has those with different gifts that enable understanding and direction for mission. Some of my more intellectual friends have said that the quest to be spiritual is just a personal quest to be happy and has a trace of self-centeredness. My reply is that the community, the church, needs diversity in order to be inclusive and have a well-rounded mission.

The point is clear, that the healthy church has these many dimensions. My goal, in the community in which I nurture my faith, is to be able to make a modest contribution. Over the years, this has been possible for me; I do have a contribution to make, and to a large extent have been encouraged to serve. What I have discovered is that I have been able to link and integrate my interests, my education, and the need of the church communities in which I have served. My interest across the years has been to gain clarity in my beliefs and to find justification for holding them and modifying them as I have gained knowledge and perspective on the needs in my community, and, indeed, the needs of society and the world in which I live.

STEP THREE: LIVING MY VOCATION

My special interest has been to understand my faith and to be able to share it with others in a way that enables and empowers them to live wisely and well in a complex and dangerous world. I have been able to engage in this ministry because I have sought to understand the perilous world in which we live, and I have been formally educated for and privately committed to this cause. My early ministry was in a university setting where knowledge was valued. I worked hard to articulate the faith and its value in the context of university life, seeking and sharing an outlook that is a responsible quest for truth, one that gave guidance and insight on how to think about values and live a responsible life. Faith must have intellectual integrity.

Later, with more education, I was able to work once again in the context of higher education where the articulation and practice of a religious faith was passively accepted, but not affirmed. It was one subject and option that should be understood, but in general it was not considered a viable option because it was generally seen as based on superstition and even, at times, as capable of being dangerous. I was a chaplain and professor across the years of my career and found great fulfillment in preparing myself well and sharing the faith option in a well-grounded way in a secular context.

My first appointment out of seminary was at a local church in a university town, and it was an ideal appointment for me, even though the denomination of the church was different from my background. They had a very strong ministry to students, and while the church itself was a bit conservative for the university community, it had a very open and welcoming spirit for students. In fact, many of the students found the clear statement of beliefs and practices in the church a valid option, living as they did in the wide-open and questioning context of the 1960s. I felt modestly at home in both settings, the university and the community of faith, and many students found a home in the church's university ministry.

I did, however, sense that my university and seminary education was not altogether adequate for the full welcome in a university setting. I sensed a need to be on an equal basis with faculty members, and I found that students in the sixties never ran out of questions. It was a challenging time in our country, with assassinations and an unpopular war. The word "existential" had crossed the waters from Sartre's Paris, and only a few dared to say that they "had the truth." Those who did were judged to be uninformed about how complex the world really is.

I left after nearly five years of service to seek the PhD, hoping I might be able to serve in a better way in the mission that seemed to be ideal for me: to discern how an intelligent faith orientation might be helpful in guiding so many students who sought answers for the most basic questions of life.

I returned from Scotland with the PhD and the knowledge that was attached to it, and was welcomed on the faculty and as chaplain, first in a small university in Atlanta, and then in a larger university in Spokane where I served nearly fifteen years. It was a good setting for me; it was church-related, and yet was open to the tremendous changes and challenges of the new world that was being born.

STEP FOUR: BEING TRUE TO MY CALLING

As I look back, I am a bit surprised that my career unfolded in ways that matched my growth and development. At no point, over the sixty years of service, did I feel that I made a mistake and made the wrong choice (not that every assignment was easy and without the adjustment to a new setting). Returning to Eugene following seminary was to enter into a ministry with which I was familiar. If there was a small amount of stress, it was being more open to alternative ways of understanding faith and being in a denomination that was conservative. Yet I had a great deal of freedom and was committed to being sensitive to an evangelical Baptist faith that was a different expression of faith than I was growing into and that seemed to me to be unable to find its way in the tremendous cultural change of the 1960s. I was loyal but knew that my career path would go in a different direction, although I was given a great deal of freedom in the campus ministry assignment. In a sense, I learned a great deal about the challenges of ecumenical ministries and being a loyal partner with those who have a different slant on how to understand and articulate the Christian faith.

In four and a half years, I was back as a student in a university setting, working on the PhD in theology at the University of Edinburgh. While New College of the University of Edinburgh worked comfortably with the Church of Scotland, it was not sectarian and served a vast and diverse population. It had a faculty that welcomed and even encouraged diversity. I learned a great deal about Christian thought and also learned how to welcome and learn from those who represented different ways of putting faith together.

Now, in my eighties, I look back and see a pattern of change and development in my life and in the way I now understand the Christian faith. I have moved to some views and starting points that now seem important but would have been controversial at an earlier time in my life, in that I served in a fairly conservative setting. I do hope that my dear friends, still holding on to a more conservative outlook, will understand my journey of faith; it has given me integrity. I find that within this frame of reference, I can easily integrate the findings of science, cosmogenesis, and human development and find great wisdom from the other great religions of the human family. I can share with my great teachers, the apostle Paul and, of course, Jesus, who modeled a shift from cultic faith orientation to one filled with freedom, conviction, and integrity. It has the following shifts and components:

1. The first is that I am inclined to understand the Bible as containing the story of the people of faith, and in this story, we are introduced to a universal and loving God. It contains a story for all of humanity. I do accept the historical scholarship that has helped us see the Bible as a human document, yet one containing the word of God.
2. I am now more inclined to understand Jesus as a first-century Jewish prophet and teacher whose life and teaching have given us a wonderful

way to be truly ethical and spiritual. I am a bit less inclined to make Jesus fit the formula of the Trinity and more inclined to follow him as a model of ethical practice and the great teacher about the life of love. The terms Savior and Lord point to the way we are saved from a harmful and destructive life and guided to a life filled with grace and truth.

3. I spend less time focused on the notion that "he died for my sins" and appeased an angry God who might otherwise send people to hell. He died because of the sins of his contemporaries, and did so with the spirit and courage of one of the greatest human beings that ever lived. His life of love and his sacrificial death make him Lord and Savior.
4. I am now more likely to welcome the views and perspectives of other religions, see them has having both the value and the danger of any human religion, and do not say that they are wrong and unable to guide their adherents to a good and spiritual life. God speaks many languages.
5. I would not start with the assumption that the views of other religions are wrong, although all religions may have some aspects that are less than noble. If a religious outlook helps humans find meaning and an ethical life, then it is serving its purpose and may be a partner with other faith traditions. It follows that those who use violence and war as a means of getting their way violate the sacred will of God.
6. I am more committed to using my faith to guide me in finding good ways to help create a more just and humane world than I am in trying to convert a person from another faith so that they might be "saved." God's love covers what might come following death.
7. I am also committed to using my faith in a loving God to inspire me to be aware that our world is threatened by our abuse of our natural environment. If our natural world is the gift of God, and if God has asked the human family to be good stewards of the earth, then we must have the equivalent of religious commitment to save our Mother Earth.
8. I do accept the science that tells how the human family came into being and the biblical story that we humans have the image of God within us. Therefore, I accept all human beings and dare not view those different from me as less than the children of God.
9. I do not know for sure that "there is life after death," but I do hope that if there is, all people, even those who are twisted and harmful, will be

restored in some way and become what God intended for all of us to be. God's love is unconditional, broader and deeper than tribal and exclusive expressions of faith.

10. I have learned across the years that love, truth, justice, and peace hold our world together, and that I need to make them the foundational values in my life and see them as the call to care for the world. I volunteered and am still at it with Jesus as my guide.

STEP FIVE: STAYING DEEPLY ROOTED ALTHOUGH I MAY MOVE SOME TOMORROW

I stay deeply rooted in my Christian faith and continue to work diligently to follow its teaching. I understand Jesus as the one who, in his life, teaching, ministry, and prophetic voice, expressed what we need to know in order to live wisely in a troubled and perilous world. I learn from many other great and gifted teachers as well, but with Jesus, I can with integrity say that I have been given a foundation on which to build my life and a calling expressed so clearly in the Golden Rule: "In everything do to others as you would have them do to you, for this is the law and the prophets" (Matt 7:12).

Jesus illustrated this universal challenge; again and again, he taught it and practiced it. It has become my life calling, although I occasionally fail. I am therefore also drawn to his teaching about the prodigal son, the story of the father who had two sons (Luke 15:11–32). The younger son asked for his inheritance, and the father gave it willingly. The younger son squandered it all in a distant country. Meanwhile the elder son continued to work diligently for his father. The younger son, feeling desperate, returned and said, "Father I have sinned against heaven and before you; I am no longer worthy to be called your son; treat me like one of your hired hands" (Luke 5:18–19). But the father, when he saw his son returning, was filled with compassion; he ran and put his arms around him and kissed him. He gave him a robe of honor and celebrated his return. The elder son was not all that happy, and said to his father that he had stayed home and served diligently. The father's love was there for both sons—for the one returning, who received forgiving love, and for the elder brother, who was reassured of the father's love: "Son, you are always with me, and all that is mine is yours. But we have to celebrate and rejoice, because this brother of yours was dead and has come to life; he was lost and has been found" (Luke 15:31–32).

I am the son of a loving Parent whose love never ceases and who always welcomes me home. As Paul reminds us, "No, in all these things we are more than conquerors through him who loved us. For I am convinced that neither death, nor life, nor angels, nor rulers, nor things present, nor things to come, nor powers, nor height, nor depth, nor anything else in all creation will be able to separate us from the love of God in Christ Jesus our Lord" (Rom 8:37–39).

WHAT IS "FORMATION"?

> Formation assumes that every person has access to an inner source of truth, named in various wisdom traditions as soul, spirit, or heart—a source of strength and guidance that is the place of truth telling within us where we know the difference between reality and illusion. The work of formation involves a quiet, focused, disciplined space—a circle of trust—in which the noise within us and around us can begin to hear our own inner voice. A personal and communal process, formation invites us to reclaim our own wholeness and vocational clarity and recognize the vital relationship between the inner life of mind and spirit and the outer life of work and service in the world.[4]

QUESTIONS FOR REFLECTION AND DISCUSSION

1. How do you find answers to life's hardest questions, such as what values are important,and how to live your life with integrity and love?
2. In what ways does Jesus guide us through his life and teachings about how to live in a dangerous world?
3. Do you have a favorite story or specific teaching in the Bible that has been helpful to you?
4. What do you find most difficult about living with integrity in the way you express your faith and care for those who are important to you?
5. Select three words that describe your deepest values.

4. From a 2006 publication of the Sacred Art of Living Center for Spiritual Formation, obtained from the Center for Courage and Renewal.

BOOKS TO CONSULT

1. Diana Butler Bass, *Grounded: Finding God in the World—A Spiritual Revolution*
2. Marcus J. Borg, *Jesus: Uncovering the Life, Teachings, and Relevance of a Religious Revolutionary*
3. C. S. Lewis, *Mere Christianity*
4. Jürgen Moltmann, *The Way of Jesus Christ*
5. N. T. Wright, *Jesus and the Victory of God*

Bibliography

Achtemeier, Paul, ed. *Harper's Bible Dictionary*. San Francisco: Harper and Row, 1985.

Aristotle. *The Basic Works of Aristotle*. Edited by Richard McKeon. New York: Random House, 1941.

Baer, Greg. *Real Love: The Truth About Finding Unconditional Love and Fulfilling Relationships*. New York: Gotham, 2003.

Bailey, J. Martin, and Douglas Gilbert. *The Steps of Bonhoeffer: A Pictorial Album*. Philadelphia: Pilgrim, 1969.

Barth, Karl. *Church Dogmatics*. 2/2: *The Doctrine of God*. Edited by G. W. Bromiley and T. F. Torrance. Edinburgh: T&T Clark, 1957.

Bass, Diana Butler. *Grounded: Finding God in the World—A Spiritual Revolution*. New York: HarperOne, 2015.

Bonhoeffer, Dietrich. *Ethics*. New York: Touchstone, 1975.

———. *Letters and Papers from Prison*. Edited by Eberhard Bethge. New York: Simon & Schuster, 1997.

Borg, Marcus J. *Jesus: Uncovering the Life, Teachings, and Relevance of a Religious Revolutionary*. San Francisco: HarperSanFrancisco, 2006.

Borg, Marcus J., and John Dominic Crossan. *The First Paul: Reclaiming the Radical Visionary Behind the Church's Conservative Icon*. New York: HarperOne, 2009.

Borg, Marcus, and N. T. Wright. *The Meaning of Jesus*. San Francisco: HarperSanFrancisco, 1999.

Bornkamm, Günther. *Jesus of Nazareth*. New York: Harper & Row, 1960.

Bourgeault, Cynthia. *The Wisdom Jesus*. Boston: Shambhala, 2008.

Chacour, Elias. *The Sermon on the Mount: An Invitation to Receive and Advance the Reign of God*. Eugene: OR, Wipf & Stock, 2025.

Chopra, Deepak. *Quantum Body: The New Science of Living a Longer, Healthier, More Vital Life*. New York: Harmony, 2023.

Connick, C. Milo. *Jesus: The Man, the Mission, and the Message*. Englewood Cliffs, NJ: Prentice-Hall, 1974.

Crossan, John Dominic. *Jesus: A Revolutionary Biography*. San Francisco: HarperSanFrancisco, 1993.

Dalai Lama. *Toward a True Kinship of Faiths: How the World's Religions Can Come Together*. New York: Doubleday Religion, 2010.

Delio, Ilia. *The Emergent Christ: Exploring the Meaning of Catholic in an Evolutionary Universe*. Maryknoll, NY: Orbis, 2011.

———. *Making All Things New: Catholicity, Cosmology, Consciousness*. Maryknoll, NY: Orbis, 2015.

———. *The Unbearable Wholeness of Being: God, Evolution, and the Power of Love*. Maryknoll, NY: Orbis, 2013.

De Rougemont, Denis. *Love in the Western World*. Princeton: Princeton University Press, 1956.

Echegaray, Hugo. *The Practice of Jesus*. Maryknoll, NY: Orbis,1980.

Ehrman, Bart D. *Jesus: Apocalyptic Prophet of the New Millennium*. Oxford: Oxford University Press, 1999.

Erikson, Erik H. *Identity: Youth and Crisis*. New York: Norton, 1968.

Ferguson, Duncan S. *Exploring the Spirituality of the World Religions*. New York: Bloomsbury Academic, 2010.

Fowler, James W. *Becoming Adult, Becoming Christian: Adult Development and Christian Faith*. New York: Harper & Row, 1984.

———. *Stages of Faith: The Psychology of Human Development and the Quest for Meaning*. San Francisco: Harper & Row, 1981.

Fox, Matthew. *Creation Spirituality: Liberating Gifts for the Peoples of the Earth*. San Francisco: HarperSanFrancisco, 1991.

Hanh, Thich Nhat. *Living Buddha, Living Christ*. New York: Penguin, 1995.

Horsley, Richard A. *Jesus and the Politics of Roman Palestine*. Columbia, SC: University of South Carolina Press, 2014.

Hutt, Rosamond. "What Are the 10 Biggest Global Challenges?" World Economic Forum, January 21, 2016. https://www.weforum.org/stories/2016/01/what-are-the-10-biggest-global-challenges/.

Jones, Edward P. *The Known World*. New York: HarperCollins, 2004.

Jung, Carl. *Modern Man in Search of a Soul*. New York: Harcourt, Brace & World, 1933.

Kee, Howard Clark. *Understanding the New Testament*. 4th ed. Englewood Cliffs, NJ: Prentice-Hall, 1983.

Keepin, William. *Belonging to God: Spirituality, Science and a Universal Path of Divine Love*. Woodstock, VT: Skylight Paths, 2016.

King, Martin Luther, Jr. *A Call to Conscience: The Landmark Speeches of Dr. Martin Luther King, Jr.* Edited by Clayborne Carson and Kris Shepard. New York: Grand Central, 2002.

Kinghorn, Warren. *Wayfaring: A Christian Approach to Mental Health Care*. Grand Rapids: Eerdmans, 2024.

Kolodiejchuk, Brian, ed. *Mother Teresa: Come Be My Light: The Private Writings of the Saint of Calcutta*. New York: Doubleday, 2007.

Kornfield, Jack. *A Path with Heart: A Guide Through the Perils and Promises of Spiritual Life*. New York: Bantam, 1993.

———. *The Wise Heart: A Guide to the Universal Teachings of Buddhist Psychology*. New York: Bantam, 2008.

Küng, Hans. *On Being a Christian*. Translated by Edward Quinn. Garden City, NY: Doubleday, 1976.

Lawrence, Brother. *The Practice of the Presence of God*. New Kensington, PA: Whitaker House, 1982.

Levison, John R. *Filled with the Spirit*. Grand Rapids: Eerdmans, 2009.

Lohfink, Gerhard. *Jesus of Nazareth: What He Wanted, Who He Was*. Collegeville, MN: Liturgical Press, 2012.

Maddow, Rachel. "Anti-Trump Protests Sweep the Country as His Approval Rating Sinks to New Lows." MS NOW, Dec. 2, 2025. https://www.ms.now/rachel-maddow-show/maddowblog/trump-approval-rating-protests-healthcare-redistricting-immigration-raids.

Meier, John P. *A Marginal Jew: Rethinking the Historical Jesus.* 4 vols. New York: Doubleday, 1991–2009.

Merton, Thomas. *Contemplation in a World of Action.* Garden City, NY: Image, 1973.

Metaxas, Eric. *Bonhoeffer: Pastor, Martyr, Prophet, Spy.* Nashville: Nelson, 2010.

Meyer, Ben F. *The Aims of Jesus.* London: SCM, 1979.

Moltmann, Jürgen. *Theology of Hope: On the Ground and Implications of Christian Eschatology.* New York: Harper & Row, 1967.

Newell, J. Philip. *Listening for the Heartbeat of God: A Celtic Spirituality.* New York: Paulist, 1997.

Nouwen, Henri J. M. *Life of the Beloved: Spiritual Living in a Secular World.* New York: Crossroad, 1992.

Nygren, Anders. *Agape and Eros.* Translated by Philip S. Watson. London: SPCK, 1953.

Pelikan, Jaroslav. *Jesus Through the Centuries.* New Haven: Yale University Press, 1985.

Post, Stephen G. *Unlimited Love: Altruism, Compassion, and Service.* Philadelphia: Templeton Foundation, 2003.

Presbyterian Church (U.S.A.). "Brief Statement of Faith." 1983. https://centernet.pcusa.org/what-we-believe/brief-statement-of-faith/.

———. *The Constitution of the Presbyterian Church.* Part 1, *The Book of Confessions.* Louisville: Office of the General Assembly, 2002.

———. *The Constitution of the Presbyterian Church.* Part 2, *The Book of Order.* Louisville: Office of the General Assembly, 2011.

Richo, David. *How to Be an Adult: A Handbook on Psychological and Spiritual Integration.* New York: Paulist, 1991.

Rohr, Richard. *The Universal Christ: How a Forgotten Reality Can Change Everything We See, Hope for, and Believe.* New York: Convergent, 2019.

Schweitzer, Albert. *The Quest of the Historical Jesus: A Critical Study of Its Progress from Reimarus to Wrede.* New York: Macmillan, 1948.

Simpson, Christopher Ben. *Modern Christian Theology.* 2nd ed. London: T&T Clark, 2016.

Snyder, Timothy. "The Logic of Destruction." Substack, Feb. 2, 2025. https://snyder.substack.com/p/the-logic-of-destruction.

Teilhard de Chardin, Pierre. *The Future of Man.* Translated by Norman Denny. New York: Harper & Row, 1959.

———. *The Hymn of the Universe.* New York: Harper & Row, 1969.

———. *Man's Place in Nature.* Translated by Rene Hague. New York: Harper & Row, 1956.

———. *The Phenomenon of Man.* London: Collins, 1955.

———. *Teilhard de Chardin Album.* Edited by Jeanne Morier and Marie-Louise Aboux. London: Collins, 1966.

———. *The Vision of the Past.* New York: Harper & Row, 1966.

Teresa, Mother. *Life in the Spirit: Reflections, Meditations, Prayers.* Edited by Kathryn Spink. San Francisco: Harper & Row, 1983.

Tillich, Paul. *The Courage to Be.* New Haven: Yale University Press, 1952.

———. *Dynamics of Faith.* New York: Harper & Row, 1958.

———. *Systematic Theology.* 3 vols. Chicago: University of Chicago Press, 1953–64.

United Nations. "Global Risk Report." 2024. https://unglobalriskreport.org.

Vacek, Edward Collins. *Love, Human and Divine: The Heart of Christian Ethics.* Washington, DC: Georgetown University Press, 1994.

Walsh, Roger. *Essential Spirituality: The 7 Central Practices to Awaken Heart and Mind.* New York: Wiley & Sons, 1999.

Weiner, Tim. *The Mission: The CIA in the 21st Century.* New York: Mariners, 2025.

Wikipedia. "Global Catastrophic Risk." https://en.wikipedia.org/wiki/Global_catastrophic_risk.

Willige, Andrea. "Five Years to Go: Are We on Track to Meet the Sustainable Development Goals?" Sept. 12, 2025. World Economic Forum. https://www.weforum.org/stories/2025/09/sdg-progress-report-2025/.

Wright, N. T. *Jesus and the Victory of God.* Minneapolis: Fortress, 1996.

———. *Paul and the Faithfulness of God.* 2 vols. Minneapolis: Fortress, 2013.

Index

www.ingramcontent.com/pod-product-compliance
Lightning Source LLC
LaVergne TN
LVHW050637100826
845148LV00011B/1892
* 9 7 9 8 3 8 5 2 6 5 1 2 1 *